This Book
Belongs To

M

What People Are Saying about

The Elect Lady
and Bishop Eddie L. Long

Bishop Long teaches us to never again doubt our value and to honor our intuitive wisdom and brilliance, our fierceness and grace. Like his beloved mother, he encourages us women—and men, too—to accept our "election" by God to create joy and meaning in our lives and lead the world toward needed change.
—Susan L. Taylor
Editorial Director, ESSENCE

It is a rare experience for me to pick up a book and find myself being immediately drawn into its pages. This one did it. It's like the story of my own life. Bishop Long, with his blatant honesty about his personal past and exposing the struggles that make us all human, makes this work an endearing pleasure that will take the reader on a roller-coaster ride of emotions, including joy, wonder, sympathy, contemplation, reflection, and encouragement. I highly recommend this book—one destined to become a classic.
—Dr. Myles E. Munroe
Bahamas Faith Ministry International
Nassau, Bahamas

Bishop Eddie L. Long has a gift for speaking to the heart of the matter, especially when it comes to understanding one's divine destiny. While most of us try to elude our election in an effort to avoid the costs, *The Elect Lady* has been written in such a way as to make claiming our call irresistible and the path to our greatest joy and fulfillment in life.

—Dr. Cynthia Hale
Sr. Pastor, Ray of Hope Christian Church

Wow…what a marvelous opportunity this new book of Bishop Eddie Long affords us! Bishop Long reaches straight into the hearts of women like me who have been elected by God, but rejected by people. Elected by God, but in a strange place—an unfamiliar place of pain, anger, disillusionment, fear, worry, and doubt because of life's experiences. Suddenly there is new hope, new strength, and new courage available because the insight given Bishop Long. Chapter after chapter is a must-read for kingdom women who are elected by God to do kingdom work, but it is also for the men who desire clarity, understanding, and wisdom to walk with God's elect women. Thank you, Elder Vanessa Long, for requesting your husband to preach this message at your Annual Women's Conference. Because you both obeyed God, millions of women are being helped, encouraged, strengthened, and appreciated!

—Dr. Wanda A. Davis-Turner
Preacher, teacher, and author

The great gift that Jesus gave to women was that He noticed, He affirmed, and He courageously celebrated the women others found invisible. In *The Elect Lady,* Bishop Eddie Long has lovingly touched the pulse and gently kissed the brow of many forgotten modern women. She is not in bright lights or on glossy magazine covers, but she may be the woman most celebrated by her Savior…and by the men who truly understand. —Claudette Anderson Copeland, D.Min.
Pastor, New Creation Christian Fellowship,
San Antonio, Texas

After decades of advocating for women, I know the issues we face. Therefore it is with a great sense of gratitude that I applaud Bishop Long for *The Elect Lady.* This book is an encouraging and empowering manual and is a must-read for every woman ready to be the "Elect Lady" God ordained her to be! —Dorothy Height
President Emeritia/Chair for the National Council of Negro Women

the Elect Lady

Life's Interruptions
Become Godly Opportunities

Eddie L. Long

WHITAKER
HOUSE

THE ELECT LADY:
Life's Interruptions Become Godly Opportunities
hardcover edition

ISBN: 978-0-88368-281-4
Printed in the United States of America
© 2008 by Eddie L. Long

Whitaker House
1030 Hunt Valley Circle
New Kensington, PA 15068
www.whitakerhouse.com

Library of Congress Cataloging-in-Publication Data

Long, Eddie.
The elect lady : life's interruptions become godly opportunities / Eddie Long.
p.   cm.
Summary: "Shows women what God can do with a yielded life as they accept His divine plan, even when it is not what they dreamed of"—Provided by publisher.
ISBN 978-0-88368-281-4 (hardcover : alk. paper) 1. Christian women—Religious life. 2. Submissiveness—Religious aspects—Christianity. 3. Providence and government of God. 4. Control (Psychology)—Religious aspects—Christianity. I. Title.
BV4527.L66 2007
248.8'43—dc22   2007009217

2 3 4 5 6 7 8 9 10 11 12 ⨅ 15 14 13 12 11 10 09 08

Contents

Introduction

You hold in your hands a work of love, a book filled with precious things from my heart that I have rarely shared until recently. Most people don't know that my mother saved my life by laying down her own best interests to tend to mine and those of my brothers—and for that we will always be thankful.

I've discovered that God has a special place, and a very special name, for women who sacrifice for their children, their spouses, their parents, and even the total strangers they meet on the street, in classrooms, at church, or on the job. These are Elect Ladies, chosen and anointed to do what few can accept and most do not.

Such personal sacrifice and self-denial is at the extreme end of the politically *incorrect* spectrum today—especially for women in this "liberated" era. (I am all for women of freedom, but my definition of true liberation comes from God's Word in John 8:36 NASB: *"If therefore the Son shall make you free, you shall be free indeed."*)

Jesus had many positive things to say about women throughout His public ministry, and it seems that for most of His three-and-a-half years leading to the cross, His ministry was financed by wealthy women who believed in Him. (See Luke 8:1–3.)

Our Lord's mother was a remarkable woman, elected by God to do the unthinkable: to give birth to God's only begotten Son and to bear the unimaginable pain of seeing her Son die on a cross. Few people ever wonder what happened to Mary *after* the cross and the resurrection, but we do know she was there in the Upper Room when the gift of the Holy Spirit descended on the 120 disciples. As you shall see, we have evidence that this Elect Lady—and many like her since that day—continued to obey the call of God and minister to others with great honor.

If you are a modern-day Elect Lady, then you are about to be blessed, encouraged, uplifted, and inspired by some precious gemstones of truth found in God's Word. May God's love enfold you as you read these encouraging words.

With devotion and gratitude for all that you do,

Bishop Eddie L. Long

Atlanta, Georgia

Chapter 1

To the Elect Lady

The young woman felt the hairs on the back of her neck stand up. She gazed into the piercing eyes of the aged holy man, but she really didn't want to hear his haunting warning about her Son and their future:

> This child marks both the failure and the recovery of many..., a figure misunderstood and contradicted—**the pain of a sword-thrust through you**—but the rejection will force honesty, as God reveals who they really are.
> (Luke 2:34–35 MESSAGE, emphasis added)

This just wasn't the way she imagined it would be.

Everything was fine until the unexpected teen pregnancy. Her fiancé wasn't the father of the child, but he still agreed to marry her in an awkward and earlier-than-planned marriage ceremony.

Her abrupt disappearance to spend several months with an older relative some distance away launched a storm of speculation back home. The tongue-wagging among the hometown busybodies only increased when she returned with obvious changes in her physical appearance that could only mean a baby was coming.

There is a unique role that only you can fulfill.

(The favorite phrase traded across tables, shared at the village market, and whispered from ear to ear at public events was "hurry-up wedding.")

Then came the emergency do-it-yourself baby delivery in a small country town far from home and separated from the rest of her family and friends.

These were the circumstances neighbors speculated on and were more than happy to repeat.

Years later, she would read a handwritten letter from someone who was her Son's closest associate in His final years on earth. It began, *"To the **elect** lady..."* (2 John 1:1, emphasis added). Although the letter did not bear her name, she knew John had addressed it to her.[1]

Mary was "elected" or *chosen* for her unique task and mission in the same manner that *you* were chosen by God for a unique role of your own that only you can fulfill.

HOW MANY WILL BE AFFECTED BY YOUR OBEDIENCE?

She was not merely appointed to an "office"; she was chosen for a mission, designated for a function, reserved for a destiny.

Her obedience, along with the lifelong obedience unto death of her Son, Jesus, would affect billions of lives and countless generations. How many will be affected by your obedience or disobedience to the Master's election?

God doesn't establish "offices" for politics' sake. He *elects* people like Mary—and ordinary people like you and me—to fulfill His own plans and purposes, to perform kingdom pursuits with eternal results.

> *God elects ordinary people to fulfill His plans.*

Don't puff and strut with pride because God elected you to fulfill a divine purpose. The apostle Paul made it clear there isn't much room for human gloating, bragging, or strutting over your election:

> *For you see your calling, brethren, that **not many wise** according to the flesh, **not many mighty, not many noble,** are called. But God has chosen the **foolish** things of the world to put to shame the wise, and God has chosen the **weak** things of the world to put to shame the things which are mighty; and the **base things** of the world and the **things which are despised** God has chosen, and the things which are not, to bring to nothing the things that are, that no flesh should glory in His presence.*
>
> (1 Corinthians 1:26–29, emphasis added)

God's calling for your life is based entirely on His wisdom and divine plan, not on your human qualifications or abilities. But *you* must also choose to yield and invest your life to His plan.

You have the power to reject your election and forfeit the blessing. You also have the power to accept your election and possess God's blessing.

THE ELECT *Lady*

AN ANOINTED MESSAGE

*"**To the elect lady** and her children, whom I love"* (2 John 1:1, emphasis added). These simple words from John to Mary unleashed a river of tears the morning I read them in the closing address of our annual women's conference. The explosive response caught me totally by surprise!

Until that morning, I had been reluctant to speak at our annual "Heart to Heart Women's Conference," thinking that it was a special privilege better served by anointed female speakers or by male speakers with proven ministries to women.

My wife had urged me to address the conference for eight years because she was convinced it would bless the ladies. When she mentioned it this particular time, I sensed that God was speaking to me through her.

When I stepped forward to deliver the message that Sunday morning, something supernatural happened as I read John's greeting from his second epistle.

> ***To the elect lady** and her children, whom I love in truth, and not only I, but also all those who have known the truth.* (2 John 1:1)

MANY LOOK BACK AT YESTERDAY WITH REGRET

The Holy Spirit began to stir the hearts of the ladies at the conference and from my congregation at New Birth Missionary Baptist Church. As the message of God's election in Mary's life unfolded, many wept openly. They represented millions of others around the world who had opened their eyes to the light of a new day that morning *only to look back* at yesterday with a tinge of regret or a sense of stinging loss.

Whether we admit it or not, most of us retain vivid Technicolor images of all of the people, things, activities, hopes*, and dreams that used to excite us when we were younger. The honest ones among us might put it this way after we wipe away our tears: "God took away my stuff and elected me to do something else."

"To the Elect Lady...."

Why did these words, written thousands of years ago, trigger such strong reactions in that thoroughly modern, twenty-first century audience?

These words offer the hope of healing and divine purpose to everyone burdened by questions of "what might have been" and "what if?" God's message through John possesses the power to release us from the memories that replay in our minds with all the paths we should have taken.

You don't choose destiny. Destiny chooses you.

I am convinced that the force of God's love and election in our lives is able to break through our false faces and plastic social exteriors. It exposes broken places inhabited by lost opportunities, disappointed expectations, and buried remnants of past betrayals we've encountered in life.

Please understand me: I have virtually no doubts that you—and anyone else who belongs to Christ—have entertained a direction or a desired destiny you *wanted* to pursue...*until God changed it in some way.*

This is the problem: You don't choose destiny. Destiny chooses you.

God sent a message to the Israelites, who were living in

slavery and exile far from home—a message that applies to each of us today through Jesus:

> *"For I know the plans I have for you," says the LORD. "They are plans for good and not for disaster, to give you a future and a hope. In those days when you pray, I will listen. If you look for me in earnest, you will find me when you seek me."* (Jeremiah 29:11–13 NLT)

If you have had some dreams that were dashed along the way, then God is speaking to you through Jeremiah's prophetic words. God has some plans—they are part of your holy destiny—and these divine plans are for good and not for disaster. They are meant to give you a future and a hope—if only you can accept your election.

John wasn't writing to a woman who "had it made." He was writing to a woman who had watched her most godly dreams seemingly dashed and destroyed in her life.

The apostle didn't specifically mention Mary's name when he started his letter with the greeting, *"To the elect lady."* However, he was the same man who gazed at the bloody and bruised body of Jesus on the cross of Calvary while standing alongside the Lord's mother.

This was the same John who heard his friend and Savior, Jesus, call to them both in the midst of His pain at the very end of His life:

> *When Jesus therefore saw His mother, and the disciple whom He loved* [John] *standing by, He said to His mother, "Woman, behold your son!" Then He said to the disciple* [John], *"Behold your mother!" And from that hour that disciple took her to his own home.* (John 19:26–27)

In His last moments, Jesus made two things clear to His mother, Mary, and to His disciple John. First, He had elected (chosen) John to cover his mother for the rest of her life on earth.

Second, He also made it clear that Mary was to cover John for life as his mother. Jesus wanted John to understand that Mary was to have authority and covering *over him* so he would be able to do what God had ordained for his life. Both of them knew the Lord was saying, "I am interrupting your life."

Most of us can't stand life's interruptions. As soon as something differs from what we had hoped or planned, we complain, "My life is out of control!" Because God's ways are not our ways, His election often appears to us as a *life interruption.*

A Change of Scenery

If you have ever attended a live play or a stage performance, then you know that surprises often come after the curtain closes on a particular scene. Many times the curtain opens to a totally new scene with different backdrops and props.

Perhaps God is putting in new props and backdrops for the next scene in your life plan. Don't be surprised if it appears to be a total interruption and change from where you came from. Take courage in the confidence that God has given you authority to cover and endure whatever comes your way. As it says in 1 Corinthians 10:13 (MESSAGE):

No test or temptation that comes your way is beyond the course of what others have had to face. All you need to remember is that God will never let you down; he'll never let you be pushed past your limit; he'll always be there to help you come through it.

Mary never expected to conceive a child *before* she was married. The Bible says she was a virgin who was *"highly favored"* by God. (See Luke 1:28.) It is safe to assume that she had the usual hopes and dreams of a young woman for a husband, a home, and children of her own—in that order. As wonderful as the immaculate conception seems to us today, it was still a difficult and permanent *interruption* in Mary's life.

LIFE'S INTERRUPTION OR GOD'S ELECTION?

Perhaps you are one of the many reading these words whose life was seemingly interrupted by the unexpected conception and birth of a child.

Have you observed a thirtieth, fortieth, or fiftieth birthday while mumbling quietly to yourself, "If I had not had Leroy or Denise, I could have done what I always dreamed I would do"? Are you feeling perpetually miserable because you are stuck in the past?

Mary's first divine interruption was more than any other woman in her time could have handled, but she had more interruptions coming. We don't hear anything about Mary's husband, Joseph, after he and Mary found Jesus conferring with the teachers in the temple at Jerusalem after He turned twelve. (See Luke 2:41–52.)

First, Mary had to deal with God's call for her to conceive a child while she was still an unmarried woman. After she had pressed through all of the challenges and was ready to enjoy the full life of a married woman with children, it seems another life disruption came her way. Although the Bible record is silent on the matter, Joseph's conspicuous absence implies that Mary had to raise her family of five sons and at least two daughters as a single mother.[2] Her plans never included the option that the husband of her dreams would die young—leaving her to face the fulfillment of her oldest Son's frightening life prophecy *alone.*

ELECTED BY GOD TO DO WHAT OTHERS WOULD NOT

You have been elected by God to endure some things that other people could not or would not. Do you want to know why some people are so miserable? Perhaps they still have not accepted what God elected them to do. And what about you? Are you still trying to fight for what *you* want to do instead of accepting what *God* has for you to do?

When God says, "I'm speaking to the elected one," your true destiny and plan may be found in only one choice. Accept God's election now and fulfill His good plans for your life.

Your deepest joy can be found where God elected you to be.

Your deepest joy and greatest power can be found in only one place—in the position where God elected you to be. Stop fighting what God has ordained for you to be, and do it.

For years I have labored with the pain of knowing that my congregation includes a growing number of wonderful women who are forced by life's disruptions—either by uncontrollable circumstances or unfortunate personal choices—to raise children by themselves and to cover households as best they can.

Many of them wish there were some help for them. They cry out and pray for mates, helpers, and counselors. These are all good desires and worthy prayers, but first God may tell them, "If you can accept where you are, if you will accept My plan for you, then I will reveal that I AM is your ever-present help in a time of need. I know your needs and desires before you even speak them to Me." (See Hebrews 4:16; Psalm 71:3; Matthew 6:8.)

I don't know if Joseph could have helped Jesus any more if he had lived to see Jesus enter His adult ministry. We know Joseph was around long enough to model true manhood and to pass on the skills of carpentry and the family business to Jesus. The Lord's neighbors remarked, *"Is this not the **carpenter**, the Son of Mary?"* (Mark 6:3, emphasis added).

GOD'S PLANS ARE BIGGER THAN YOU CAN IMAGINE

There are times when someone moves out or is pushed out of the equation of our lives (gently or otherwise).[3] The Bible only speaks positively of Joseph, but for some reason Jesus entered His adult ministry apart from His earthy guardian's presence.

God will place women over men when those women possess something vital they must speak over their lives. Stop complaining that your grandma raised you! She may not have been the ideal parent to your way of thinking, but she made sacrifices for you. Be thankful for her presence in your life. You have much to be thankful for because you've made it this far. Thank God for the blessings He's placed in your life.

God is saying to countless Elect Ladies across this nation, in effect,

Stop fighting Me, Elect Lady. I know you feel your life is ruined because you didn't get the American Dream. You have the power to open your mouth and whisper the things of God to man, woman, boy, and girl!

Things may not be going the way you planned, but I say *to the elect lady and her children whom I love,* "You may have had big plans, but if you had done *those things your heart was set on,* you would be dead. You wouldn't have the spirit that you have now. You wouldn't have realized My full salvation."

Some of you need to drop the "poor me" attitude, lift your voice, and rejoice. You may be able to say, "I didn't have much, but my children always were fed! None of my children landed in jail."

YOU HAVEN'T YET SEEN HOW GOD WILL BLESS YOU

Elect Lady, you are not like so many other women. You aren't trying to "catch" a vision for something you are not. You realized long ago, "He touched me, and He loves me. I *know,* because I can look at my children. I know the love I feel for them, and God loves me even more. I know I want the best for them, and God has made a perfect plan to give the best to me." The Lord says to you, in essence,

Elect Lady, you can deal with the fact that I changed your course 180 degrees. You have already *settled* the issue—you accept the fact that I love you. Some people only want to prosper in the accumulation of things and gain man's approval. But you want to prosper in My love, and to share it with others.

Elect Ladies aren't like other women. They understand that having their entire lives interrupted by God is the catalyst that will speed them into their destinies.

Mary didn't choose her destiny; she *yielded* to it and *accepted* it. Do you battle bitterness at times? Do you wake up on certain mornings (or every morning) saying to yourself, "If it weren't for these children..."?

God says to every faithful and obedient parent in such times of despair, "You haven't seen how these children are going to turn around and bless you! They will take care of you, and these children will not let you die in an old folks' home. They are going to rise and call you *blessed*; you have not seen it come to pass...*yet*."

Mary yielded to her destiny and accepted it.

This is what is so amazing to me about John's letter to the "elect lady"— this apostle opened his second epistle with a personal address to a woman and family that he had been personally called and elected to cover *as if they were his own family*.

THIS MESSAGE SPEAKS FROM CENTURY ONE TO TWENTY-ONE

In effect, this church leader was saying, "You are still standing, even after all of the tribulation, disappointment, heartbreak, and betrayal!" This letter spans the centuries; it speaks as loudly to twenty-first century families as it did to Mary's family in the first century.

Anyone who looks closely at the families and other people in their lives will tell you that a lot of difficult and tragic events have happened in the lives of a lot of people—and only a few are standing with their lives and souls intact.

It may seem that I've chosen this particular text in 2 John to gear this book toward women, but in truth there is a message here for *everyone* whose life has been or may be interrupted by the unexpected and unwanted—that goes for female, male, young, and old.

Yet, in my own heart, I think it is significant that the apostle John addressed his letter to an *"elect **lady**."* In my lifetime, I've seen more women's lives interrupted than men's.

Perhaps it is because the level of true manhood is lower in our nation, or maybe the modern American woman is more focused on a man's looks and flashy personality, and on escaping her childhood home. It could be both causes and a host of others simultaneously. Regardless of the causes, we see more and more young women giving birth to children, only to see the men in their lives run away from their responsibilities as fathers, husbands, providers, and protectors. Some start their families within the bond of marriage, but the majority of them do not.

As I prepared this message, I wept over the images sweeping through my mind and heart. I was thinking of the mother who spent her whole life raising her children, only to enter her old age with grown children who seem totally ungrateful for her selfless sacrifice of love. I thought of my own mother, who raised four sons virtually alone.

I thought of the many people in the church who have said publicly, "I will *never* go down the road of sin," but they went down that road anyway—all the way to the end. I've watched far too many of them reach the place where things got too rough for them to handle in their own strength and they fell (and didn't get up).

It seems that there is no end to the roadblocks and obstacles that appear in our lives and change our expectations. Dreams are good things to have, but from our earliest days we should understand that our lives are not our own, for we've been *"bought with a price"* (1 Corinthians 6:20, 7:23). Wise parents carefully train their children to seek God's plan for their lives and to live according to God's Word while seeking His kingdom *first*. When we do that, we give God freedom to plant His kingdom plan in our hearts, making His desire *our* desire from the very beginning of our lives. It is good to remember that God said,

> *And everyone who has left houses or brothers or sisters or father or mother or wife or children or lands, for My name's sake, shall receive a hundredfold, and inherit eternal life.*
> (Matthew 19:29)

WILL SHE GIVE UP HER CHILDHOOD DREAMS?

If you haven't noticed, little girls tend to have great dreams for their lives (and so do little boys…but often with a significantly different slant).

My wife and I are trying to teach our little daughter how important it is to clean up her room and keep it that way. I just gave up one day and went in to clean it up myself.

Taylor's room was cluttered with Barbie and Ken dolls, and it revealed a great deal about her dreams of how her life will be. I am convinced that in some way and at an appointed time, God will somehow interrupt those dreams.

How will she be able to give up her dreams as a child to dream something else as an adult? Have we prepared her properly for the way of the Lord, even if it takes her in a different direction, far from her childhood dreams and expectations?

My wife and I know that Taylor has a very special call on her life, and our prayer is that she will accept whatever God has for her and enjoy His supernatural provision for that destiny.

In writing this book, I recalled the great debate I had with my wife. As I mentioned earlier, she wanted me to close out the annual women's conference and I really didn't want to. When I finally accepted her invitation, I began to study the Word of God for a timely message. In the process, I began to look at women in the church, in marriage, and even in the unsaved world.

MY WIFE EXPERIENCED A DIVINE INTERRUPTION

The heart of this message was birthed in a revelation about the challenges that my wife has faced since our marriage. When I met my wife, we both had personal and private perceptions about life and marriage. The truth is that you don't really know what those perceptions are until you actually say, "I do," and start to live together.

There was no way that I could have explained to her what it would be like to be my wife, to be married to the pastor of a growing church that I knew was destined to impact our state and nation.

The way of the Lord may take you from your childhood dreams.

My wife had dreams of having her husband come home after working from 8 a.m. to 5 p.m. every weekday. She looked forward to building memories of picturesque weekends in the park together. Those weren't wrong or selfish dreams, but she was about to experience a divine interruption in her life.

Vanessa is a very quiet and thoughtful person. You might say she is a very private person. When she married me, Vanessa

23

discovered that everything she had "inherited" when she joined her life to mine was totally opposite from what she had wanted and expected.

The last thing she wanted was to be thrust into a public arena and to be forced to cope with a hectic and unpredictable schedule. Vanessa is very methodical. Everything has to be in place, and change bothers her because she really enjoys the routine of a more "orderly" life. She married a man who enjoys pioneering things and "calling those things which are not as though they were."[4]

For my part, I found it very difficult to stand by and be her husband but *not* her pastor. It is nearly impossible to "turn off" the anointing and focus of pastor simply because you enter the front door of your house. Yet, it is difficult to pastor your spouse. Why? It is a fact that many of your spouse's challenges will stem from *you*!

I was trying to address a woman who had entered a new relationship with me carrying a whole set of dreams, goals, and aspirations in life. She felt that our marriage was a significant move in that direction and that she was finally getting what she wanted after a lot of disappointment earlier in her life.

It didn't take long for Vanessa's eyes to open up, and she began to understand that everything she had dreamed about had *not* come to pass. God had radically changed her life and disrupted her direction. Now she had to wrestle with a difficult choice: Would she spend the rest of her life being bitter, or would she follow the truth found in the old expression that says, "When life serves you lemons, make lemonade"?

THEY GAVE UP THEIR DREAMS FOR THE SAKE OF OTHERS

As I thought about Vanessa's experience, I realized that all of this applies on a much broader scope. I found that throughout human history, there have been countless numbers of great women who have given up their lives, their dreams, and their planned careers for something else of even greater worth.

Many of the most remarkable women in history had great dreams, great ambitions, and great desires to move in a higher dimension in life and personal achievement. Many American women have longed for and dreamed of having their own slice of the proverbial "American pie." They wanted the opportunities and privileges in American life that everyone was promised, but they woke up to find themselves in a totally different situation. They weren't able to choose their destiny, destiny chose them.

When I read the apostle John's greeting, *"To the elect lady,"* I thought of Mary the mother of Jesus and of all the suffering and sacrifice she experienced in her life. I thought of what her sacrifice has meant to me, personally, and to everyone else who has even been touched by the life, death, and resurrection of her Son, Jesus Christ.

Then my mind flashed with images of various people who have made sacrifices for others, especially the women I've known who gave up their dreams for the sake of others.

I have noticed that the greatest women I've known (including my own mother) had a deep desire to go after their dreams. They had the intellect to achieve great things, and they had the personal drive and gifting to accomplish whatever they put their minds to. Yet, in the course of life, some of them married and experienced bitter and unwanted divorces. Others were abandoned along the way. Virtually all of them gave birth to children whom they ended up raising alone.

As single parents, they were left to struggle privately with the care, provision, and nurture of the children. For many of them, things happened suddenly and unexpectedly; but in every case, they were left "holding the bag." How would they ever be able to make ends meet?

These remarkable women somehow survived, raised their children, and even began to take responsibility to stand in the gap in their churches. This was in contrast to others in similar circumstances who became discouraged and never made it into a caring church family. Some of them became suicidal or turned to alcohol, drugs, sex, or other self-destructive lifestyles. They didn't understand that there are times when God totally interrupts your life because of His destiny for you and that, when life interrupts your plans, He is there to renew and restore His purposes for you.

> *God has given you grace to do whatever you put your mind to.*

THE BAND OF THE DISRUPTED

Have you pursued things that God never chose or intended for your life? (I think *all* of us have.) Have you ever said to yourself, in a moment of pain or bitter disappointment, "If it hadn't been for…I could have…"? Welcome to the band of the disrupted.

The crucial problem isn't that you sometimes take unfortunate detours or speak self-pitying things in moments of pain—the most important issue is what you do *afterward*.

Will you get better or grow bitter? Will you join the forgotten fallen, or will you still be standing in the end with trophies of victory in your hand?

If you have been interrupted on the road of life and you have found it difficult to recover, God is saying to you right now, *"To My Elect One, I have given to you the grace to do anything you put your heart and mind to in accordance with My good purposes for you."*

The book you are reading was written because I know—on the deepest personal and emotional level—what it is to point to an Elect Lady and say, "I am here because *you* were there for me in the midst of your own worst crisis. You stayed when it would have been easier to go. You are my hero."

In the next chapter, I will introduce you to one of the greatest women in the world. I sense that her story may be similar to your own story.

ENDNOTES

1. Some scholars say this letter was written to the church; others believe it was sent to some unknown woman held in high respect long after Mary had died. In my opinion, the epistle of 2 John was addressed to Mary. John's affectionate greeting to *"the elect lady and her children"* is accompanied by a very special closing statement: *"The children of your elect sister greet you"* (v. 13). There is circumstantial evidence that John's mother may have been Salome, sister to Mary. (See Matthew 27:56; Mark 15:40; John 19:25.) This would make John a first cousin to Jesus, and would make it very likely that John was writing to

Mary, his adopted mother and the birth mother of Jesus.

2. Jesus had four half-brothers—James, Joses, Judas, and Simon—as well as "sisters" (meaning at least two), according to Mark 6:3.

3. The household of Saul was removed from the equation of Israel's future. Jonathan voluntarily removed himself from the throne of Israel through a binding covenant with his friend, David. Jonathan's father, King Saul, was removed by force. (See 1 Samuel 20 and 2 Samuel 1, respectively.) Nabal, the brutish husband of Abigail, refused to honor God's anointed king (David), so God brought his life to a premature end, and his widow married David. (See 1 Samuel 25.)

4. See Romans 4:17. This is an attribute of God that seems to "rub off" on men and women called to pioneer new churches, ministries, outreaches, and works of God's kingdom.

* Special note: The hope we're discussing here is equivalent to wishful thinking except where we have quoted the Bible. The hope discussed in Scripture is a firm, confident expectancy.

Chapter 2

If You Leave Me, I Will Die

My hero never finished sixth grade.

When her mother got sick, my hero had to leave school and stay home to care for her. Then she married my daddy and became a preacher's wife. Every other year after that, for the next several years, she had a child.

My mother came to grips with her pain one day and realized that her life was literally messed up. She faced the fact that everything she had dreamed, and everything she had ever hoped for, just wasn't there. Her only joy in life was her four boys (I have to confess I was her "mama's boy").

I remember seeing her shoulders heaving that day as she cried uncontrollably. She was hysterical.

I'll never forget the way she said over and over again, "My life is over, my life is over, my life is over...." Mom had finally come to the point where she had just given up.

On that day, in Mom's forty-fifth year, she decided to leave. She knew she had little hope of keeping us if she left, because she would have to live on her own with no support from Dad. I didn't know how she was going to live, because she was cleaning other folks' houses to make money at the time. I was still a little boy then, but I knew Mom was serious. It was over.

She couldn't stop weeping as she packed her things in a suitcase. You could tell she had left the marriage and our house already in her heart and mind, but God interrupted her life.

I remember grabbing Mom in a desperate, boyish hug as she cried uncontrollably in the bathroom. I begged her not to leave. "If you leave me, I will die!" I still get emotional when I think about it. I begged Mom not to leave because I really felt that, if she left that day, I would die. I just knew I couldn't handle it emotionally. Regardless of what I am today, on *that* day I was a little boy who desperately needed his mother.

MOM SAVED MY LIFE THAT DAY

For some reason, she heard my plea and stopped packing. She sat me down on the bed and just hugged me. I believe that, by her decision, she saved my life that day in countless ways.

The crisis in Mom's life rose through her relationship with Dad. Even though my daddy was a preacher, he was not the type of person who demonstrated unconditional love. Some of his controlling ways only made matters worse.

He was very chauvinistic in many ways. Mom had to cook whenever Dad got home. Even if he walked in at two o'clock in the morning, Mom was expected to get up and cook something and serve him.

I love and honor my father, who is with the Lord today, but in those early years he demanded that everything go his way. He made life miserable for everyone in the house. Dad never allowed my mother to get a driver's license, so she had to wait for him to take her places and pick her up, or else she had to catch a bus. If she got home too late, or if she missed the bus, he tended to explode in anger toward her. For some reason, he was a very jealous man, although my mother never gave him any cause or reason for his suspicion.

After Mom stopped packing on that fateful day long ago and set aside her own pain to comfort me, she never looked back. She stayed and faithfully covered her sons, even though her circumstances did not improve.

My mother stayed and faithfully covered her sons.

At times, my father had bouts of rage when he would grab a gun and chase my mother around the house threatening to kill her. Those times scared all of us.

Then came a day I will never forget. My brothers and I were much older, and Dad went through one of those anger fits again. He grabbed the gun we'd seen so many times before and started to threaten Mom. But this time, we all rose up and grabbed him. There must have been something about the way we looked at Dad that stopped him in his tracks. He knew that we were no longer little boys.

When we warned him not to threaten Mom again, he put down the gun and left the house. From that day on, it never happened again. We had come of age, and Dad knew we were ready and willing to take care of the woman who had taken such good care of us.

It is especially painful to share with you the rest of Mom's story.

In the years that followed, I grew up and God helped me make my own way in the world and in the ministry. Meanwhile, there was some reconciliation at home.

Eventually, my dad reached the point where he realized he was too old to run around, and he started spending more time at home. He soon realized that he had done some very wrong things, and he apologized in his own way. As he mellowed and genuinely tried to make up for his wrongdoing, he and Mom began to enjoy life as never before. Then he had a stroke.

For the next four years, Mom had to care for Dad, which made her a little angry. Just when she had finally received another glimpse of hope for her marriage and her future, Dad got sick. Once again, Mom had to put aside her dreams and personal plans to care for her husband. Then he died.

Mom came to stay with me after Dad's death. Within a couple years, we began to notice that Mom was acting strangely. Then she woke up one day and said, "I want to go home." (We later learned that Mom was experiencing the first stages of dementia, which explained her strange actions and frequent memory lapses.)

As I was driving her back to Charlotte, North Carolina, Mom suddenly asked me to take her to my younger brother's house. So I stopped at Larry's house, and Mom got out. From that day on, Larry's home was her home.

My brother has seven wonderful daughters, and they have been my mother's faithful caregivers ever since the day she first arrived. My brothers and I always told Mom that we would never put her in a retirement home, so she would never have to worry about that.

MY MOTHER DOESN'T EVEN KNOW WHO I AM

Today, I can't call her on the telephone because she doesn't know what to do with the phone anymore. In fact, my mother doesn't even know who I am. I know the pain felt by millions of people whose loved ones suffer from Alzheimer's or similar diseases of the memory and mind. These conditions seem to rob their victims of key parts of their personalities along with many of their fondest memories.

I know what it is like to look at the shell of the woman who gave birth to you, who battled to keep you, to cover you, to love you, and to give you a chance at success in life—all the while just hoping for any sign that she will remember who you are and why you love her so much.

Because my heroic mother denied herself to cover me, I am touching lives all over the world. She is still alive, but she doesn't recognize me; she can't remember most of the things we shared together in previous years, and she can't personally receive the honor for her selfless investment.

The Lord opens doors of opportunity for me to minister to people all over the world each year, but if Mom hadn't paid such a high price early in my life, then I might have had a hard time even traveling out of my city.

It may sound strange to you, but my mother's willingness to cover me with her motherhood years ago laid the foundation for me to extend spiritual fatherhood to countless people and entire church congregations around the world today.

She Covered Me So I Could Cover Others

While working on this book, I went to London, England, to speak at a major conference and participate in a book-signing event as an author. Hundreds of people from many nations and different continents lined up for blocks to meet me and receive an autographed book, but at the same time I could still see myself as a little boy being comforted by a mother in crisis.

God chose a humble woman to make me who I am today.

God has done a great work in my life, and He alone is worthy to receive the glory for what He has done. Yet, I also know He chose a humble, brokenhearted woman—an Elect Lady—to help make me who I am today.

The crowd was so large at the London book signing that the allotted time ran out before we ran out of people, and I had to stop signing books. People from Holland, Sweden, and Africa waited as long as two hours to reach the table.

Men from Africa came up to hug me and say that I had become the only father they had ever known, even though I had never met them. It was a humbling experience, and through it all I kept thinking about God's faithfulness—and about the special Elect Lady He placed in my life to cover me.

God Credits Mom's Heavenly Account for Every Soul

Despite the pain of my mother's ongoing battle with dementia, I find incredible joy in my conviction that God

34

credits Mom's account every time a soul is saved or someone is healed through the ministry He has given to me. Mom's heavenly account expands every time I am able to preach a message that blesses people and nations.

Why? My mother was an Elect Lady who remained steadfast in selfless love. She modeled the love of Jesus by being faithful to pay the price while in the midst of her own personal hell. When she wanted to run for cover herself, she held her ground to cover the precious ones God had placed in her womb and in her life. I am here today because *Mom* was there when God asked her to trust Him and cover her children.

The sacrifices made in my life by Jesus Christ and by my mother motivate me to push beyond every boundary and obstacle for the sake of God's kingdom. Mom's life has not been spent in vain; her private personal sacrifices for her children will not be wasted. They help keep me going.

Partly because Mom covered me when I was vulnerable and needy, I've been able to help build a hospital in Nairobi, Kenya, and serve on the board of trustees at a major university I was supposedly too stupid to attend. Millions have heard the gospel around the world and received encouragement to go on—all because of the Elect Lady God put in my life.

What is our right response to the women (and men) in our lives who have made these kinds of sacrifices? How should we respond to the mothers, wives, and grandmothers who went beyond the call of duty to cover and carry others?

NEVER FORGET, AND BE THERE WHEN THEY NEED YOU

I will begin with two simple suggestions: First, we must never forget the price they paid on our behalf. Second, as much as is possible, we should be there for them when they need us in their later years.

We live in an era when many people dispose of their elderly parents as casually and thoughtlessly as they dispose of their fast-food containers. Once the health or financial state of a parent begins to put a demand on time or resources, many will sign over their parents' homes and possessions to the lowest bidder among available retirement homes. *What if those parents had taken the same attitude when their offspring were in need as children?*

> *Jesus cared for His mother, even from the cross.*

Once again, Jesus set the gold standard. He exercised tender care for His mother, even at a time when He was undergoing the greatest test ever experienced by any living being—on the cross of Calvary.

Although His body was racked with unspeakable pain and His heart was breaking with the weight of the sins of the world, Jesus still took time to care for the welfare of the Elect Lady in His life.

Look again at this passage in John 19:

*Near the cross of Jesus stood his mother, his mother's sister, Mary the wife of Clopas, and Mary Magdalene. When Jesus saw his mother there, and the disciple whom he loved standing nearby, he said to his mother, "**Dear woman, here is your son**," and to the disciple, "**Here is your mother.**" From that time on, this disciple **took her into his home.** Later, knowing that **all was now completed**, and so that the Scripture would be fulfilled, Jesus said, "I am thirsty."*
(John 19:25–28 NIV, emphasis added)

THE MISSION ISN'T COMPLETE UNTIL THE ELECT LADY IS COVERED

This is a picture of a godly Son fulfilling His final duty to the Elect Lady in His life. Jesus refused to consider His mission complete until He had provided for the future and security of His mother. That is why, immediately following Jesus' assignments to Mary and John, the Bible says, *"Knowing that all was now completed..."* (John 19:28).

Did you notice how John reacted after Jesus said, *"Here is your mother"*? The verse in the original Greek might be translated, "From that time on, this disciple *took her into his own."* Most translators add the word *house* or *home* to help us capture the meaning, but one insightful translator interpreted it as John "took her into his own keeping."[1]

This is what my brother and his daughters have done. They took Mom into their own keeping.

At the very minimum, there are millions of Elect Ladies around our nation and the world who might be able to say with my mother, "I've walked out my election. In the end, I was able to mature four boys into men."

This is even more amazing when you understand that my father was never really there. On those occasions when he did come home, he would get a report from Mom and then start beating us. He never nurtured us; he was a harsh disciplinarian because that was all he ever knew from his own father.

MOM PRAYED OVER US NIGHTLY— INDIVIDUALLY AND COLLECTIVELY

We were all normal boys, so from time to time we definitely committed offenses and pulled stunts worthy of punishment.

THE ELECT *Lady*

We needed discipline, but it was Mom who raised and nurtured us day in and day out. She loved us, she spanked us when we needed it, and she prayed over us every night—individually and collectively.

In the end, none of us ever went to jail. Not one of us ever got in trouble or tried drugs or fathered children out of wedlock. Each of us learned early what good values are, so it was a natural thing for us to make a commitment among ourselves to always take care of Mom. In our eyes, Mom was and is the virtuous Proverbs 31 woman. As her children, we have risen up to call her blessed.

As her children, we have risen up to call her blessed.

At the same time, Mom met the qualifications for God's blessings and provision. Psalm 127 says,

> *Like arrows in the hand of a warrior, so are the children of one's youth. Happy is the man who has his quiver full of them; they shall not be ashamed, but shall speak with their enemies in the gate.* (Psalm 127:4–5)

My mother was faithful to accept her election in God, and because she willingly laid down her hurts to cover us, the Lord has seen to it that she will never lack anything or worry about her needs being met.

NOW IT IS OUR TURN

Mom cared for us and covered us until we were grown men, and now it is our turn. We and our families will care for and cover Mom the rest of her days. When she needs things, we buy them for her. When she wants to go someplace, we take her.

It has been this way ever since we first got our driver's licenses as young men. One of my earliest assignments was to be "on call" every Saturday. That was the day assigned to me for Mama's cab duty, so I remained ready and waiting to take Mom where she wanted to go.

Even as Mama's health continues to fail, we are determined never to "put her away." We still honor her, and we are careful to preserve her dignity in big and small ways. My nieces are faithful and loving toward her.

For example, as the dementia grew more intense, Mama forgot how to comb her hair, but nevertheless her hair is combed every day. She is bathed and fed every day; and she is surrounded by people who love her, including her sons, her daughters-in-law, and all of her grandchildren.

Mama's doctor says she is extremely healthy physically, but her memory has faded except for select memories that she enjoys each day. For our part, we make sure she is in familiar settings, surrounded by pictures of her past.

On any given day, Mama may spend her time wandering through certain events from yesterday, such as going to work or talking to family members long gone. She is nearly always happy and jolly. She smiles, she laughs, she often talks about things from the past (even though we don't always know what she's talking about), and sometimes she looks for her husband.

This Elect Lady never got to go back to school after she left to care for her mother. Again, she cleaned folks' houses to make money for most of her adult life, and dementia robbed her of memory just when she had finally reached the place where she could start to enjoy life. It is the job of my four brothers and me to remember for her.

THE ELECT *Lady*

WHAT DID THIS ELECT LADY ACCOMPLISH?

Even as I preach to thousands in person or on television, my mom doesn't know it's Sunday. Yet, once more, I believe God is recording in her book the name of everyone whose life is transformed and saved through my ministry.

What did this Elect Lady accomplish? She covered sons who collectively grew up to cover their own families, and millions of other people, with their love, their ministries, and their faithfulness.

Long ago, I cried out in tears and desperation, "If you leave me, I will die!" This woman laid aside her pain, her fears, and her frustration to cover me and preserve my future. You are reading this book because this Elect Lady heard my cry and paid a high price to answer it.

Is someone crying out to you, "If you leave me, I will die!"? What cross has God called you to bear? Has God interrupted your life? How will you answer His summons to destiny?

ENDNOTES

1. Curtis Vaughan, gen. ed., *26 Translations of the New Testament* (Grand Rapids, MI: Zondervan Publishers, 1967), 427, citing from *The New Testament in the Translation of Monsignor Ronald Knox* (New York: Sheed and Ward, Inc. and Burns and Oates, Ltd., 1944; with the kind permission of His Eminence, the Cardinal Archbishop of Westminster and Burns and Oates, Ltd.).

Chapter 3

Arrested and Interrupted by Destiny

Rejected. Misunderstood. More easily disowned than believed. How many Christians in our churches today would have given Mary the benefit of a closer look or a second chance? Would *you* have been open to the possibility that her story was actually true?

Would we be more interested in pointing out the appearance of sin in Mary's life, or in drawing her close to pursue the truth and bring reconciliation? (Or restoration, if our worst suspicions were true?)

We should be thankful that Joseph was no ordinary man and that he listened and obeyed when God intervened to divert disaster in the nick of time. Sometimes, I wonder if *we* would have done as well as Joseph did that day.

At times, the big things of God arrest and interrupt the small things in our lives. This God we serve seems to like invading tiny villages and visiting unknown "nobodies" to plant His purposes in the earth.

Outward circumstances just aren't *reliable* proofs about God's presence or absence in a situation. It *looked* as if God was *not* present in Mary's awkward circumstances as an unwed mother—yet *He was!*

> It may look as if God isn't present, but He is.

How can that be? Why would God allow Mary to face such public embarrassment? And why would He allow Himself to get tangled up with the messed up lives of adulterers and murderers (such as David), prostitutes (such as Rahab),[1] and the demon-possessed (such as Mary Magdalene)[2]?

God warned us that He is not a "tame" God who asks for human opinion or conforms to our ideas of how things should be! This is the almighty God who said,

> *For my thoughts are not your thoughts, neither are your ways my ways, saith the LORD. For as the heavens are higher than the earth, so are my ways higher than your ways, and my thoughts than your thoughts.* (Isaiah 55:8–9 KJV)

Why should we be surprised that God would choose an unknown Jewish teenage girl—the last person anyone would suspect—to bring His only Son into the world?

Just how many religious leaders of that day—or of ours, for that matter—would have recognized God's hand behind such questionable circumstances? We know from the Bible record that precious few even had a clue. It all looked like just so much "foolishness."

Looks can lie. The apostle Paul said, regarding the cross of Christ,

> *This "foolish" plan of God is far wiser than the wisest of human plans, and God's weakness is far stronger than the greatest of human strength.* (1 Corinthians 1:25 NLT)

Likewise, the human mind tends to recoil at the thought of God's using what *appears* to be an "illegitimate birth" to bring righteousness to our world. For Mary to give birth to Jesus, the only begotten Son of God, no human male could be involved in the process. She *had* to conceive her child through the miraculous action of the Holy Spirit prior to her marriage.

Modern American society tends to "wink" at unwed mothers, but Mary's day was unlike today. Pregnancy outside of wedlock was a total disgrace that put her at risk for immediate public execution.

Her fiancé was the key—if he cried "foul" and exposed her unexplained pregnancy, then Mary could have been stoned to death. Instead, the Holy Spirit again arrested natural human thought processes and intervened in Joseph's life through a dream. The Bible says,

> *But while he thought on these things, behold, the angel of the Lord appeared unto him in a dream, saying, Joseph, thou son of David, fear not to take unto thee Mary thy wife: for that which is conceived in her is of the Holy Ghost.*
> (Matthew 1:20 KJV)

THE ELECT *Lady*

When God elects a woman to do His will and places her at risk of rejection, He will also arrest and intervene in the lives of others who have the power to begin blessing and covering her. It may not happen instantly, but God *will* make a way where there seems to be no way.

Why does God "arrest" His elect ladies and the people around them to reveal His election in their lives? Most of the time, you and I couldn't handle the full revelation of God's call on our lives. We couldn't manage the total sacrifice required, the total risk involved, or the total favor and blessing that will come through it all. No, God's will is done through one obedience, one sacrifice, and one step of faith at a time.

> *God's will is done through one step of faith at a time.*

It *cost* a great deal for Mary and Joseph to obey God.

- We don't read a detailed account in the Scriptures about the murmuring and backstabbing gossip that probably raged through the village behind their backs. However, since that kind of human behavior has dominated virtually every known society in human history—and since we know the people with whom Jesus grew up were fully capable of rejecting God and misunderstanding Him—it is almost certain it happened there in Mary's lifetime.

- We have no written record of the scornful conversations that may have dominated the atmosphere at the local public well. No one but God knows how deeply Mary was rejected by the other women in her village.

- Based on what we *do* know about the Jewish customs and laws of her day, Mary could have been viewed with disgrace much of her life—even among her closest childhood friends.

Yet, none of that mattered because Mary, alone, was elected to give birth to the Son of God in fulfillment of ancient prophecies. With great honor and great historic events come great responsibility and sacrifice.

Mary experienced pain on virtually every level of human existence.

She submitted herself to God's will and felt the pain of social rejection, isolation, and misunderstanding from family members, friends, and even her own fiancé.

Later, she experienced the physical pain of labor and delivery when she gave birth to God's Son in Bethlehem.

Finally, she felt a searing pain of the soul pierce her heart when He was crucified. The seed of this pain was planted even as she received a spiritual blessing! It happened when she and Joseph took Jesus to the temple in Jerusalem to dedicate Him as a firstborn son. A man named Simeon was alerted by the Holy Spirit to go to the temple at exactly the same time, and he delivered a powerful prophecy over Jesus—and a painful word to Mary as well.

And when the parents brought in the Child Jesus, to do for Him according to the custom of the law, [Simeon] took Him up in his arms and blessed God and said: "Lord, now You are letting Your servant depart in peace, according to Your word; for my eyes have seen Your salvation which You have prepared before the face of all peoples, a light to bring revelation to the Gentiles, and the glory of Your people Israel."

45

*And Joseph and His mother marveled at those things which were spoken of Him. Then Simeon blessed them, **and said to Mary His mother**, "Behold, **this Child is destined for the fall and rising of many** in Israel, and for a sign which will be spoken against (yes, **a sword will pierce through your own soul also**), that the thoughts of many hearts may be revealed."* (Luke 2:27–35, emphasis added)

Even in the midst of Mary's pain, God was bringing about the birth of a far greater thing. When you look at your life or some especially difficult circumstance, you may wonder, "Why me? Isn't there someone else who is stronger, smarter, richer, more patient, or better equipped for the job? Why did God arrest me and interrupt my life to accomplish His will?"

None of us can "choose" the best plan for ourselves. Only God can do the choosing, and only God can bring His will to pass through your life. And He rarely, if ever, spells out the details of where His call will take us.

Paul put it all in perspective when he explained,

*Remember, dear brothers and sisters, that few of you were wise in the world's eyes, or powerful, or wealthy **when God called you**. Instead, **God deliberately chose** things the world considers foolish in order to shame those who think they are wise. And **he chose those** who are powerless to shame those who are powerful. **God chose** things despised by the world, things counted as nothing at all, and used them to bring to nothing what the world considers important, so that no one can ever boast in the presence of God.* (1 Corinthians 1:26–29 NLT, emphasis added)

If you die in childbirth, you will never realize what all the pain was for. Don't die in the process of giving birth to destiny.

Don't give up. Refuse to allow a day of intense pain or disappointment to lead to wrong decisions. Avoid surrender to a fateful weakness, producing a lifetime of regret.

When God intervenes in your life, you've entered a season of divine rearrangement. What appears to be an interruption is actually a divine adjustment. He isn't *changing* the reason for your birth—He is *realigning* your life to line up with His original plan conceived long before you were born!

In the distraction of your pain and the confusion of transition, you might *miss the real reason for your season.* No one should miss the reason for which he or she entered the world.

God elected you for something no one else can do.

Understand that God loves you so much that He elected you to do something that He didn't trust anybody else to do. Once you understand that fact, it won't matter how many other people simply misevaluate and dismiss you, put you down, or refuse to give you proper credit for your calling.

Be encouraged—we've just described what Jesus had to endure—*and He was perfect!*

This promise from God helps, as well, when the Lord arrests you and interrupts your life for a divine intervention. According to Paul, this is something any of us can hold on to in times of unbearable struggle and hopelessness:

> *No temptation has seized you except what is common to man. And God is faithful;* **he will not let you be tempted beyond what you can bear.** *But when you are tempted, he will also provide a way out so that you can stand up under it.* (1 Corinthians 10:13 NIV, emphasis added)

47

Mary didn't know what she was getting into when she told the angel of God, *"Behold the handmaid of the Lord; be it unto me according to thy word"* (Luke 1:38 KJV). Sometimes we don't see the fruit of our suffering or labor in our lifetime. At other times, it is delayed until much later in our lives than we ever dreamed.

Mary stepped onto a holy roller-coaster ride that brought surprise after surprise to her life. As a pure, young maiden, she had dreams of marrying Joseph and raising a family, just like countless other young women around her. But she became pregnant by the Holy Spirit, was accepted by her fiancé anyway, then had her Son in a stable and was told that grief would pierce her heart in the days ahead.

She had been told that, through her Son, the sins of many would be rolled away. But did she ever dream she would watch Him stagger through Jerusalem's crowded streets, covered in blood and carrying a cross on His shoulders? Did she ever dream that He would be crucified on a Roman cross at the personal demand of Israel's high priest?

Even when it was clear Jesus was about to die, when He told John to take in Mary as his own mother, neither one of them really knew what would happen three days later. I don't think they really anticipated the resurrection. They never thought they would see Him again, let alone see Him and then "lose" Him to the heavenly realms.

The good news is that Mary *did* see Jesus again, and at this moment she dwells with Him in the very presence of the Father.

Sometimes mothers who have been interrupted by destiny start praying for prodigal sons and daughters, but they never see the *answer* to those prayers in their lifetimes. Those children don't get saved until *after* their mothers have already gone to their reward in heaven.

Yet, when that happens, perhaps these praying parents, grandparents, aunts, uncles, and siblings get to join the vast "cloud of witnesses" Paul talked about in the letter to the Hebrews, and see God's timely answer to their prayers.

> *And what more shall I say? For the time would fail me to tell of Gideon and Barak and Samson and Jephthah, also of David and Samuel and the prophets: who through faith subdued kingdoms, worked righteousness, obtained promises, stopped the mouths of lions, quenched the violence of fire, escaped the edge of the sword, out of weakness were made strong, became valiant in battle, turned to flight the armies of the aliens. Women received their dead raised to life again. And others were tortured, not accepting deliverance, that they might obtain a better resurrection. Still others had trial of mockings and scourgings, yes, and of chains and imprisonment. They were stoned, they were sawn in two, were tempted, were slain with the sword. They wandered about in sheepskins and goatskins, being destitute, afflicted, tormented; of whom the world was not worthy. They wandered in deserts and mountains, in dens and caves of the earth. And all these, having obtained a good testimony through faith, did not receive the promise, God having provided something better for us, that they should not be made perfect apart from us. Therefore we also, **since we are surrounded by so great a cloud of witnesses,** let us lay aside every weight, and the sin which so easily ensnares us, and let us run with endurance the race that is set before us, looking unto Jesus, the author and finisher of our faith, who for the joy that was set before Him endured the cross, despising*

the shame, and has sat down at the right hand of the throne of God. (Hebrews 11:32–12:2, emphasis added).

Are you wrestling with the consequences of failure, mistakes, or sin in your life? Do you feel trapped, as if your circumstances have robbed you of all your dreams, with no hope for a "real life"?

Perhaps you have been arrested and interrupted by God. It really boils down to your trust in God. Will you actually trust Him with what is most precious to you?

Are you willing to trust God that His good will for you may be to find a good spouse and have children, to go into the ministry, or to start your own business? The real challenge of trust comes when your faith must cover several *years* without seeing any progress in the direction of your dreams. Can you trust Him all those years when things *don't* happen?

> *God can even use your mistakes for His glory.*

Thousands of young ladies collide with crushing crisis in their early teens when they find themselves pregnant and virtually alone. Most of them go the way of the world and follow the easy counsel of their unsaved friends or believe the misleading claims of the government-financed abortion industry and abort their children.

Although God certainly did not orchestrate their sin, He will use their mistakes for His glory. All life is precious, and He knew your baby's days before he or she was born and had a divine plan for that little one's life. When a child is aborted, the good that its life was meant to accomplish dies too.

Whether we abort our children or abort the dream of God planted in our hearts, the pain of failure can start when we are young and may affect the future for generations to come.

Abortion takes an innocent life created by God, and it is not right. At the same time, many women struggle with the pain and sorrow of abortions for years afterward. Some live with such crippling guilt that they even contemplate suicide.

The Bible says *all have sinned*, and we *all* need the cleansing blood of Jesus to wash away our sins. (See Romans 3:23; 1 John 1:7.)

If you or one you love has had an abortion, confess it to the Lord, ask Him to forgive you, and allow His mercy and grace to totally remove your sin and give you a new start in life.

The apostle John explained it all far better than I could when he wrote,

> *My dear children, I am writing this to you so that you will not sin. But if you do sin, there is someone to plead for you before the Father. He is Jesus Christ, the one who pleases God completely. He is the sacrifice for our sins. He takes away not only our sins but the sins of all the world.*
>
> (1 John 2:1–2 NLT)

The apostle Paul was first known as Saul, the zealous Jewish Pharisee, the "Christian killer." He imprisoned and murdered many Christians with the full blessing of his nation's religious leadership until God arrested him in his tracks. Saul *thought* he was doing God a favor, but the Lord interrupted his life direction and sent him in the *opposite* direction. Saul accepted his divine election; then he made the deaths of the Christians he had killed count for something far greater!

Saul became known as the apostle Paul, and his life and ministry in Jesus' name affected multiple generations for good—even though he had previously done wrong.

If you have gone through abortions, borne children out of wedlock, sold drugs, hurt others, or made foolish decisions that landed you in prison or in a rehabilitation program under court order, I urge you to accept your election by God! Understand that He has arrested you for divine reasons.

THE WOMAN AT THE WELL

As we look at Mary's divine interruptions, you may be saying, "But Mary was highly favored in God's eyes. She didn't do the things that I've done. I've made mistakes, and I've sinned. Does God really want to use me?"

The answer is yes! God doesn't want His children to sin, but if you have confessed your sins, He can use them to reach someone else. You may have done some awful things, but look toward the place He wants to bring you now.

As an example, look at Jesus' conversation with the woman at the well. Jesus was traveling through the region of Samaria, and He got tired and sat by a well outside the city of Sychar to rest while the disciples went into the town to buy food. A Samaritan woman came to draw water, and Jesus asked her, *"Will you give me a drink?"* (John 4:7 NIV).

> *The Samaritan woman said to him, "You are a Jew and I am a Samaritan woman. How can you ask me for a drink?" (For Jews do not associate with Samaritans.) Jesus answered her, "If you knew the gift of God and who it is that asks you for a drink, you would have asked him and he would have given you living water." "Sir," the woman said, "you have nothing to draw with and the well is deep. Where can you*

get this living water? Are you greater than our father Jacob, who gave us the well and drank from it himself, as did also his sons and his flocks and herds?" Jesus answered, "Everyone who drinks this water will be thirsty again, but whoever drinks the water I give him will never thirst. Indeed, the water I give him will become in him a spring of water welling up to eternal life." The woman said to him, "Sir, give me this water so that I won't get thirsty and have to keep coming here to draw water." He told her, "Go, call your husband and come back." "I have no husband," she replied. Jesus said to her, "You are right when you say you have no husband. The fact is, you have had five husbands, and the man you now have is not your husband. What you have just said is quite true." "Sir," the woman said, "I can see that you are a prophet. Our fathers worshiped on this mountain, but you Jews claim that the place where we must worship is in Jerusalem." Jesus declared, "Believe me, woman, a time is coming when you will worship the Father neither on this mountain nor in Jerusalem. You Samaritans worship what you do not know; we worship what we do know, for salvation is from the Jews. Yet a time is coming and has now come when the true worshipers will worship the Father in spirit and truth, for they are the kind of worshipers the Father seeks. God is spirit, and his worshipers must worship in spirit and in truth." The woman said, "I know that Messiah" (called Christ) "is coming. When he comes, he will explain everything to us." Then Jesus declared, "I who speak to you am he." (John 4:9–26 NIV)

There are several things to notice from this passage. First of all, Jesus knew everything about the woman. He knew who she was, what she had done, and that she was living with a man who wasn't her husband. But He offered her the living water of life.

Second, let's look at the woman's response.

Then, leaving her water jar, the woman went back to the town and said to the people, "Come, see a man who told me everything I ever did. Could this be the Christ?"

(John 4:28–29 NIV)

She believed what Jesus told her and went to tell others about Him. Jesus interrupted her life that day. No doubt, her dreams for her life had not turned out the way she wanted. After all, she had had five husbands, and the man she was living with was not her husband. Whether her husbands had died or divorced her, she obviously hadn't had an easy life. People in the village probably whispered about her and spread rumors that she couldn't keep a man, that she wasn't a good person. And then she met Jesus.

Jesus came to the woman at the well where she was. He met her in her disappointments and betrayals. He knew everything about her, and instead of condemning her, He showed her forgiveness and a better way to live. As a result,

...many of the Samaritans from that town believed in him because of the woman's testimony, "He told me everything I ever did." So when the Samaritans came to him, they urged him to stay with them, and he stayed two days. And because of his words many more became believers. (John 4:39–41)

The woman at the well became a great evangelist. She brought crowds of people to Jesus, and they believed. God had a greater destiny for her than she could have ever imagined.

Make your life count! Allow almighty God to turn your life around. Don't let the deaths of your aborted children be in vain. Raise the children God gave you to be champions for Christ in their generation. Make connections for the cross instead of for a drug deal. Make your prison stay a missionary assignment and bring God's light into that place of darkness and despair. Allow the Holy Spirit to rehabilitate you so you can lend a helping hand to others in God's name.

Put God in total control of your life, and He will turn your pain and sorrow into *fuel* to feed the fire of His anointing and strength in your heart and life.

Act now. *"Behold, now is the accepted time; behold, now is the day of salvation"* (2 Corinthians 6:2). Don't put it off until it's too late. Pray this prayer with me right now.

> *Lord, please forgive me for the wrong things I've done and the people I've hurt along the way. I turn away from my old way of life, and I surrender my life to You right now. You arrested me because You love me, and I accept Your election in my life.*
>
> *Turn my life around right now, in Jesus' name. I trust You with my tomorrows, and I trust You for the strength and ability to do Your will in the days ahead.*
>
> *Thank You for a fresh start. This moment marks a turnaround, a divine change of direction, in my life. In Jesus' name, amen.*

My life has just turned around because I've accepted my election by God!

Your life has just turned around. Take a moment to worship the Lord, and then tell yourself this truth once again.

ENDNOTES

1. Read about Rahab's amazing life in Joshua 2 and 6, Hebrews 11:31, and James 2:25.

2. Mary Magdalene's name appears twelve times in the New Testament. Twice, the Bible specifically notes that Jesus cast seven demons from her. (See Mark 16:9; Luke 8:2.) Luke's gospel tells us that Jesus and the twelve disciples were accompanied by several women who had been "healed of evil spirits and infirmities" and that Mary was just *one* of these women.

Chapter 4

I Don't Remember the Last Time I Woke Up Happy

Any good doctor is careful to prepare patients for the process of healing. If you have surgery, it is normal for your surgeon to warn you about what to expect when you come out of anesthesia, how you are likely to feel, and what to watch out for over the next few weeks.

The same is true when you accept your election by God. Your life will make an instant turnaround in the spirit realm in that moment, but you need to understand how things may go in your *daily life* when God is at work.

You should have a picture of some of the challenges that may crop up, and of how they may make you feel. You must be forewarned about what God's Word says concerning key challenges likely to confront you. Why? Satan can always be counted on to try any way possible to steal, stop, or spoil what God is doing in your life! (See John 10:10.)

Many times, things will seem to get worse just before they get better.

The human body is one of God's greatest teaching tools for us. Feverish body temperatures reach their highest sustained peak just before they break. (This was widely understood before aspirin and nonaspirin painkillers became so popular.) Why? The Lord designed your body with the ability to "turn up the heat" on viruses and bacteria. Most of your body's cells can handle higher temperatures, even though this produces discomfort for you. Many infectious organisms die when the body's internal temperature reaches fever pitch. Fever is one of your body's "atom bomb" measures against infection.

Many people are shocked to learn that what they thought was a nightmare of a life—an existence seemingly lived at feverish pitches of pain and suffering—was actually part of a blessed dream of God. They were temporarily fooled by their difficult circumstances and extreme election. There are many examples of this pattern in the kingdom of God and in His Word.

NO AMOUNT OF LOGIC COULD EXPLAIN AWAY THE OBVIOUS

There was no way possible to "explain" Mary's seeming predicament to the natural mind. No amount of logic could have improved her situation or explained away what must have seemed obvious to her neighbors and family members, or to the religious world. Her situation was unique—how else would you describe the first time in history that a woman became pregnant without the presence and reproductive cells of a man?

Again, Mary was probably seen as an unwed, pregnant woman in a land and culture where adultery or fornication were sins punishable by death. At the very least—if Joseph had followed through with his plan to *"put her away secretly"* (Matthew 1:19)—Mary would have escaped death but would have been doomed to lifelong social exile as an unmarried mother and a disgraced public outcast.

To most people, Mary's life looked like a nightmare careening toward a tragic ending—*but God had a plan and the power to fulfill His vision.*

God had a plan and the power to fulfill His vision.

It took Joseph's obedience to God's vision to complete the process—he had to be willing to take on some of Mary's shame by being linked for life with a suspected "early pregnancy" that people assumed was caused by sex before marriage. But God was faithful. Even though Mary and Joseph couldn't see the "big picture," they were obedient, and God led them step-by-step for His higher purposes.

DAVID'S NIGHTMARE WAS GOD'S CAREFULLY CRAFTED DREAM

David was probably content with his life as a young shepherd boy because it was all he had ever known. The fact is that most of us would consider his existence a nightmare.

He was the youngest of a large family of sons, and he was stuck out in the "back 40" and given the job of shepherding sheep. That task was normally reserved for the lowliest of slaves or hired hands. When important things happened, all of the sons were called in for the special occasions—*except for David*. It seemed as if David was an unwanted son, or that he didn't matter in the eyes of his father and brothers.

He and his whole family would soon discover that his nightmare was God's carefully crafted dream. Even so, things got *worse* before they got better in David's life, despite a few positive moments.

It appeared that he was even robbed of some of those positive things—including his wife (her father, King Saul, gave her to another man), his home, his position of honor as a national hero, and his opportunity to worship God before the ark of the covenant (it was under King Saul's control).

David's faith was tested over a number of years filled with danger, misunderstanding, unjust persecution, and great hardship. Yet David pressed even deeper into God's presence through prayer, praise, and worship, while clinging to God's prophetic word for his life until it finally came to pass. (See 1 and 2 Samuel.)

RUTH'S TRIALS AND TEARS LED HER TO GOD'S GREATNESS

Ruth's life had all the makings of a nightmare in motion. It began when a family moved to her hometown from another country that was dying in the grip of drought and famine. The patriarch of the family died unexpectedly, leaving his widow stranded with her two adult sons in Ruth's country.

The mother decided to stick it out since there was nothing to go home to, and Ruth ended up marrying one of her sons and settling down. The other brother married a woman named Orpah. Over the years, neither woman bore any children.

Then, lightning struck twice in the same place. Both sons died unexpectedly, as their father had before them, instantly transforming the status of Ruth and Orpah from young married women to young widows without inheritance or provision.

"Ruth, can you remember the last time you woke up happy?"

The death of her sons also left Naomi totally without support or home among a foreign people. She was distraught and abandoned in a far land, with no place to live and no hope for the future.

I wonder if, during those dark days, Naomi ever turned to her daughter-in-law and looked into her tearstained face to say, "Ruth, can you remember the last time you woke up happy? Because I can't." Imagine that, in the conversations that occurred after those painful burials, all three women revealed their hearts.

> *Then they lifted up their voices and wept again; and Orpah kissed her mother-in-law, **but Ruth clung to her**. And she said, "Look, your sister-in-law has gone back to her people and to her gods; return after your sister-in-law."*
> (Ruth 1:14–15, emphasis added)

Naomi's heart was turning back home to Bethlehem, where she'd heard the drought had broken. Orpah's heart was right where it had always been—firmly rooted among her people and land. Yet Ruth's heart had been totally transformed from that of a Moabite woman into that of a devoted daughter, and a servant of Naomi's God by faith.

RUTH TRANSFORMED COVENANT COMMITMENTS FOR CENTURIES

The way Ruth expressed her devotion has transformed covenant commitments among Jews and Christians for centuries. Her unforgettable words have often been "borrowed" for marriage vows around the world.

> *But Ruth said: "Entreat me not to leave you, or to turn back from following after you;* **for wherever you go, I will go; and wherever you lodge, I will lodge; your people shall be my people, and your God, my God. Where you die, I will die, and there will I be buried. The LORD do so to me, and more also, if anything but death parts you and me.**" (Ruth 1:16–17, emphasis added)

The practical part of your mind may be thinking, *That's touching, but it still looks more like a nightmare than a miracle.* There are families created by man, and there are families created by God. Both are important, but the second category is supernatural. The Bible says,

> *A father of the fatherless,* **a defender of widows,** *is God in His holy habitation.* **God sets the solitary in families; He brings out those who are bound into prosperity;** *but the rebellious dwell in a dry land.* (Psalm 68:5–6, emphasis added)

God's election transformed the future for both women, and it may transform your life as well. Naomi was an elect woman, anointed to withstand the pressures of outliving her husband and her children.

RUTH AND NAOMI RETURNED IN COVENANT COMMITMENT

Ruth was also an elect woman, anointed by God to withstand the sorrow of premature widowhood and to reaffirm her family covenant commitment to her mother-in-law. Because she accepted her election and never looked back or shrank from this commitment, she also gave birth to part of the greatest dream of God.

When Ruth and Naomi returned to Bethlehem in covenant commitment, God directed their steps and led them to Boaz, a distant relative of Naomi. Through a series of events orchestrated by God, Boaz married Ruth; when Ruth conceived a child, she dedicated him as Naomi's grandson, giving him the same name and privileges as if his father were Naomi's son.

Heat in your life can purify your heavenly vision.

Ruth's selfless gift preserved her first husband's ancient family line and properties, assured Naomi's future in her old age, and planted Naomi's family in the earthly bloodline of Jesus Christ, the Messiah. (Boaz and Ruth are named in the genealogy of Jesus given in Matthew 1:5.)

If you don't remember the last time you woke up happy, then look for the heat in your life. In the natural world, heat often brings out impurities in such things as silver, gold, petroleum, plastics, steel, and crystals. It may be working in the same way to purge the dross—the cares and concerns of this world—and to purify your heavenly vision.

THE ELECT *Lady*

THE DAILY PROCESS OF PERSONAL DEATH AND RESURRECTION CAN HURT

God's transforming work in your spirit is instantaneous, but the transformation of your thinking, of your relationships, and of your life situation nearly always lags behind because it is in these areas that we need to *partner* with God through obedience. The daily process of personal death and resurrection in these areas can hurt—in fact, it *usually* produces pain and discouragement.

Remember, success depends on your ability to *trust* God with your life—even when the desert season has begun and there is no water in sight! Since the enemy of your soul *never* wants you to wake up happy, he schemes day and night to steal away every word from God you have ever heard. This is what Jesus was talking about in His parable of the sower:

> *And when a great multitude had gathered, and they had come to Him from every city, He spoke by a parable: "A sower went out to sow his seed. And as he sowed, some fell by the wayside; and it was trampled down, and the birds of the air devoured it. Some fell on rock; and as soon as it sprang up, it withered away because it lacked moisture. And some fell among thorns, and the thorns sprang up with it and choked it. But others fell on good ground, sprang up, and yielded a crop a hundredfold." When He had said these things He cried, "He who has ears to hear, let him hear!"*
> (Luke 8:4–8)

The disciples didn't understand the meaning of this parable right away, even though they had been with Jesus "up close and personal." So they asked Him what it meant, and He explained why it was so important.

64

*Now the parable is this: **The seed is the word of God.**
Those by the wayside are the ones who hear; then the devil
comes and takes away the word out of their hearts, lest they
should believe and be saved. But the ones on the rock are
those who, when they hear, receive the word with joy; and
these have no root, **who believe for a while and in time
of temptation fall away.** Now the ones that fell among
thorns are those who, when they have heard, go out and **are
choked with cares, riches, and pleasures of life, and
bring no fruit to maturity.** But the ones that fell on the
good ground are those who, **having heard the word with
a noble and good heart, keep it and bear fruit with
patience.*** (Luke 8:11–15, emphasis added)

Are you tired of listening to sermons, messages, and prophetic words about "perseverance" or "toughing it out" through the fires of trials and tribulations? Don't surrender to fatigue. Perseverance—through faith—is the only way.

FIVE QUALITIES OF WINNERS WHO SUCCEED DESPITE OBSTACLES

According to Jesus, there are *five qualities* that mark people who win and succeed in His kingdom despite obstacles:

1. You must *hear* the Word of God in whatever form it comes to you: the written Word (the Bible), the prophetic word (spoken to you or over you through the prophetic gifts operating in people as a confirmation to what He's been saying to you), or the inward word (where you sense God speaking to your spirit, in a way that lines up with His written Word—what God calls the inner *"unction"* (KJV) or *"anointing"* in 1 John 2:20).

2. You must hear with *"a noble and good heart."* That means your heart is honest and full of good things. God doesn't have to move out a lot of junk just to make room for His gift to you.

3. You must *keep* the message or Word of God. That means you must *seize it, hold it down, protect it, treasure it, and conceal it inside your heart!*

4. Your goal in every area of life should be to bear good fruit. Trust God for good fruit in your marriage or family relationships, on the job, in the marketplace, and in your finances. God is always looking for fruit on His vines.

5. You must do these things with *patience,* or what *The Amplified Bible* describes as "cheerful, hopeful endurance"!

The Message Bible sums it up this way: *"But the seed in the good earth—these are the good hearts who seize the Word and hold on no matter what, sticking with it until there's a harvest"* (Luke 8:15).

STICK WITH IT UNTIL YOU SEE A HARVEST IN YOUR LIFE!

You can see a harvest in your life if you don't give up.

Even if you are saying, "I can't remember the last time I woke up happy," you *can* see a harvest in your life *if* you cooperate with Him in faith and don't give up. So stick with it until you see a harvest in your life!

Are you one of those who has been dealing with depression until today? Have you been sleeping more than usual, but feeling just as exhausted when you wake up as you did when you went to bed? Has your capacity to deal with problems disappeared or been significantly reduced recently? What is your mind saying right now? Are you saying, "I can't *help* it! I just can't deal with it like I used to. Don't bring me another thing—I can't handle it"? Are you taking medication for depression but still feeling depressed?

Put your faith and trust in God. He has the power and the will to say, "That day is over!" Step into faith with Him and experience the power of joy flowing through the darkest passages of your life.

Today, you may say, "I don't even remember the last time I woke up happy." But tomorrow, if you seize the grace to accept your election by God, then you just might be screaming with joy! Something supernatural occurs when your mind, body, and spirit all go in the same direction, in sync.

The state of depression is *not* the native state of the born-again Christian! Even though we may experience *temporary* dips in our emotional state due to challenges with illness, loss, financial crises, or other life difficulties, depression should never become our permanent environment. There is too much hope, faith, peace, and joy in the life of Christ for that!

Chapter 5

Search for Significance in Your Crisis (Never Make It Your Home)

There are moments when the divine call comes to the saved and the unsaved alike: "Where are you, Adam? Where are you, Eve? Are you in the place and purpose I dreamed for you?" (See Genesis 3:1–9.)

I believe divine destiny is buried in the soul of *every* man and woman on earth, whether they call on the name of the Lord or not.

A deep longing and desire resonates in their inner being, as if a silent voice persistently tries to wake them up and tell them, "Come on board. There is something I have called you to do. There is something I have chosen you to accomplish!"

God pictures our predicament with incredible clarity in the calling of young Samuel. We are like that young boy, asleep in the thick darkness without a clue, when suddenly the very voice of God awakens us in our spiritual twilight.

> *Meanwhile, the boy Samuel was serving the* LORD *by assisting Eli* [the high priest]. *Now in those days messages from the* LORD *were very rare, and visions were quite uncommon. One night Eli, who was almost blind by now, had just gone to bed. The lamp of God had not yet gone out, and Samuel was sleeping in the Tabernacle near the Ark of God. Suddenly, the* LORD *called out, "Samuel! Samuel!" "Yes?" Samuel replied. "What is it?" He jumped up and ran to Eli. "Here I am. What do you need?" "I didn't call you," Eli replied. "Go on back to bed." So he did. Then the* LORD *called out again, "Samuel!" Again Samuel jumped up and ran to Eli. "Here I am," he said. "What do you need?" "I didn't call you, my son," Eli said. "Go on back to bed."* **Samuel did not yet know the** LORD **because he had never had a message from the** LORD **before**.
>
> (1 Samuel 3:1–7 NLT, emphasis added)

We don't always realize we are hearing God's voice because we automatically assume He would never speak directly to us.

SAMUEL STILL HADN'T HEARD FROM GOD FOR HIMSELF

Young Samuel listened to his mother, Hannah, tell the story of his miraculous birth over and over again until he

69

could recite it word for word! (See 1 Samuel 1:1–2:11.) But still he hadn't heard God for himself.

You may think, *The preacher hears God all the time, but no one else does.* God speaks to each of us, but we don't hear or recognize His voice very well. Most of what people understand about God they have heard from second- and third-party sources.

Yet, once you hear Him and answer, everything begins to change inside you. I never thought I'd be doing the things I'm doing today until I learned to hear God's voice.

At one point, I was a recently divorced dad with no job and no prospects. Even my ministry dreams had been dashed because I'd been told a divorce amounted to a death sentence pronounced on any ability or privilege to stand behind a pulpit and preach the gospel.

God speaks to us, but we often don't recognize His voice.

I've since learned that God sees things differently.

It is true that He hates divorce, because He says so. (See Malachi 2:13–16.) It is also true that when God chooses to do so, He fills His pulpits, thrones, and appointed places with saved and transformed murderers like Paul, saved adulterers like David, saved drug addicts, saved gangsters, and even saved seminary students!

In one case, He filled the pulpit at New Birth Missionary Baptist Church with a saved divorced man named Eddie, and then He blessed the work beyond Eddie's wildest dreams.

IT WAS THE CHRIST IN ME WHO MADE A DIFFERENCE

When I began to hear God's voice and obeyed Him, fulfillment filled my life. It was because I was touching somebody else with God's love and hope. I was doing something in Christ's name and power. It was the Christ in me who made a difference in human lives and destiny.

Can you see a deeper meaning in this? *Everything God does in your life and mine goes far beyond us!*

I think every man and woman is looking for something to live for, a burning purpose of significance, whether they are saved or not!

Christ in me makes a difference in lives.

Many of them discover the Lord's love in moments of crisis because that is the only time many people will finally discard their "pretend lives" and seriously try to define who they are.

Even in the church, most men and women mistake motion and busyness for mission and purpose. Many people with pure motives and wonderful intentions fill their calendars with meaningless "X's," marking the "orderly" waste of time in their lives.

Routine is normal in most lives, and we devote the majority of our lives to the rote repetition required to keep body and soul together.

We marry, we give birth, we raise our children, we work, we sleep, we play, we eat, and we even try to slip in a memorable event from time to time. (Even "the ministry" is mostly long days and nights of routine duties and hard work with a few brief high moments and dramatic services interspersed.)

71

Do You Want Purpose and Destiny or Meaningless Motion?

However, a routine based on purpose and destiny in pursuit of God is *dramatically* different from a routine filled with meaningless motion and energy expenditure totally apart from God's direction and power.

When we live in a world divorced from divine destiny, we live meaningless lives.

How many people do you know who spend most of the days in their week doing things they absolutely hate and dread?

Millions of people around the world seem to merely "live for the weekend." They try to squeeze every pleasure and moment of excitement from their small slice of "real life" from Friday night through Sunday night (often with the "help" of large amounts of alcohol, drugs, and hard partying).

On Mondays, they nurse their throbbing heads and do what they can to hide the visible side effects of their weekend binge, reluctantly returning to jobs they barely tolerate while dreading life as usual.

Either no one cared enough to tell them or they refuse to realize that at the end of their lives, when they draw their last breath, *they will have spent most of their existence on earth* dreading what they do each day.

That would be my ultimate nightmare. It's tough enough to arrive at the end of the day and discover that I've wasted even one opportunity to fulfill my destiny.

Where Am I and Where Should I Be?

The saying goes that "time waits for no man," and I have been immersed in the cold realities of midlife. I've begun to examine my life with a fresh intensity and determination.

I've discovered that I have not accomplished some of the key things God called me to do. I've been in constant conflict with myself about where I am and where I should be.

Everybody has to come face-to-face with the truth sometime: "This is not the way I planned it." Even if the process is painful, embrace the pain and face the truth. Then, release the promise of the Lord in your life:

> *And we know that God **causes all things to work together for good** to those who love God, to those who are called according to His purpose.*
> (Romans 8:28 NASB, emphasis added)

"All things" includes the good things *and* the bad things that come our way. God doesn't send bad things our way, but He certainly *causes them to work together for good* in our lives.

Crisis can help you discover more about who you are and why God elected you. Remember: *You always have a choice in crisis.* Unfortunately, too many of us seem to get stuck there!

King David was well acquainted with crisis. He had to pass through *"the valley of the shadow of death"* many times in his transition from his father's sheepfolds on the backside of Bethlehem to the king's palace in Jerusalem. He described his passage through a dark valley in Psalm 23:

> *The LORD is **my shepherd**; I shall not want. He maketh me to lie down in green pastures: he leadeth me beside the still waters. He restoreth my soul: he leadeth me in the paths of righteousness for his name's sake. Yea, **though I walk through the valley of the shadow of death, I will fear no evil: for thou art with me; thy rod and thy staff they comfort me.** Thou preparest a table before me **in the presence of mine enemies**: thou anointest my head with oil; my*

cup runneth over. Surely goodness and mercy shall follow me all the days of my life: and I will dwell in the house of the LORD for ever.   (Psalm 23:1–6 KJV, emphasis added)

Rather than closely follow our Shepherd's rod and staff as He walks us right through *"the valley of the shadow of death,"* we irrationally choose to "tabernacle" or set up our tent in the middle of our sorrows and fears!

We lie down submissively and prepare to surrender to circumstance in the very shadow of our crisis, even though the almighty God Himself is at our side!

If you allow God to teach you, He will show you how to make crisis work *for you* instead of *against you.*

A CRISIS POINT CHANGED HANNAH'S LIFE

Hannah had every right to be bitter. This Old Testament wife lived under the heart-wrenching social system of the ancient Middle East, where it was common for men to have more than one wife. (God didn't encourage it, but it happened in ancient times.)

Hannah's husband loved her, but she had been unable to conceive a child and she was getting older. Meanwhile, her husband's other wife had given birth to numerous sons and daughters. The situation reached a crisis point that changed Hannah's life and affected the destiny of Israel.

And when the day came that Elkanah sacrificed, he would give portions to Peninnah his wife and to all her sons and her daughters; but to Hannah he would give a double portion, for he loved Hannah, but the LORD had closed her womb. **Her rival, however, would provoke her bitterly to irritate her, because the LORD had closed her womb.** *And it happened*

year after year, as often as she went up to the house of the LORD, she would provoke her, so she wept and would not eat. Then Elkanah her husband said to her, "Hannah, why do you weep and why do you not eat and why is your heart sad? Am I not better to you than ten sons?" Then Hannah rose after eating and drinking in Shiloh. Now Eli the priest was sitting on the seat by the doorpost of the temple of the LORD. And she, **greatly distressed***, prayed to the LORD and* **wept bitterly.**
(1 Samuel 1:4–10 NASB, emphasis added)

You can become overwhelmed, entrapped, or just plain stuck in crisis. The longer the crisis or problem continues, the deeper the anger, cynicism, or rage becomes. It seems to me that the *worst* thing that could happen is for you to become *resigned to your crisis.*

YOU WERE NOT CREATED TO TOLERATE A LIFE OF INSIGNIFICANCE!

Don't be fooled. The Creator God, the Master Designer of all things, did *not* create you and save you just so you could tolerate a life of insignificance! He called and anointed you to be the head and not the tail, to be above and not beneath. (See Deuteronomy 28:13.)

God created you to change your world despite impossible odds.

Nowhere in the Bible does God say we were created to be lifelong *victims* of our circumstances! He gives His Elect Ladies the ability to turn around their circumstances and change the world through their lives and their children *despite* impossible odds!

It is *not* normal for you to live in a state of chaos, distress, or slavery to lack, disease, or abuse of any form. Jesus said,

*I am the door; if anyone enters through Me, he shall be saved, and shall go in and out, and find pasture. The thief comes only to steal, and kill, and destroy; I came **that they might have life, and might have it abundantly**.*

(John 10:9–10 NASB, emphasis added)

RECURRING CRISES REVEAL DEEP PROBLEMS

Beware if the same crisis comes around again and again in your life. If you find yourself hooked up with an abusive spouse, alcoholics, drug-dealing manipulators, or chronically depressed friends over and over again, then you have a problem in serious need of a solution!

Hannah learned how to turn her crisis into a triumph. She committed her problem to the One who is able to transform any situation. She shared her heart's desire with God and promised it to Him.

And she, greatly distressed, prayed to the LORD and wept bitterly. And she made a vow and said, "O LORD of hosts, if Thou wilt indeed look on the affliction of Thy maidservant and remember me, and not forget Thy maidservant, but wilt give Thy maidservant a son, then I will give him to the LORD all the days of his life, and a razor shall never come on his head."...Then [Hannah and her family] arose early in the morning and worshiped before the LORD, and returned again to their house in Ramah. And Elkanah had relations with Hannah his wife, and the LORD remembered her. And it came about in due time, after Hannah had conceived, that she gave birth to a son; and she named him Samuel, saying, "Because I have asked him of the LORD."

(1 Samuel 1:10–11, 19–20 NASB)

76

JESUS WILL REVEAL THE *SIGNIFICANCE* IN YOUR CRISIS

Jesus is *your* solution right now. He possesses absolute power and authority to set you free and give you a brand new life. If you turn to Him with *everything* in your life, then He will reveal the *significance* in your crisis and show you how to come out of it!

He promised this to all of us when He launched His ministry with these ancient words from the prophet Isaiah: *"The Spirit of the LORD is upon Me, because He has anointed Me to preach the gospel to the poor; He has sent Me to heal the brokenhearted, to proclaim liberty to the captives and recovery of sight to the blind, to set at liberty those who are oppressed"* (Luke 4:18–19).

Whatever you tolerate will continue in your life.

This is God's promise to you. Anything less than life at this level of freedom is *unacceptable!*

Are you sick and tired of tolerating mistreatment, poverty, ignorance, and slavery to the opinions and limitations imposed by others? Good! God has been waiting for you to stand up and call upon His name.

Often, He cannot or will not act until you get sick and tired of your situation and ask for His help. He will intervene once you get to the point where you have had enough.

When God first gave me this message on "The Elect Lady," I noticed that the Holy Spirit moved upon the women who heard it and gave them great hope. God's Word changed the perspective of many of the women, who were actually God's Elect Ladies.

Don't be surprised if the things you hear God whispering to your heart are *contrary* to what your friends are saying! The truth is that you've been elected by God to do the impossible. You have been chosen to persevere through things that would have caused other people to throw up their hands and throw in the towel of surrender long ago. You are anointed to stand with dignity in a place where most of the people around you would collapse in defeat.

At the end of the day, how will you answer these questions of the soul?

- Did I accept what God told me?

- Have I stood with Jesus and said, "I am despising the shame of the cross God called me to bear for the joy set before me"? (See Hebrews 12:2.)

- If there is a greater joy that lies beyond my pain today, then can I capture the joy that lies beyond this task He called me to do?

- If I have faced the fact that my life is not going the way I wanted it to go, have I finally accepted the direction *God* wants me to go?

- Have I received the joy that God wants to give me when I go in His direction? Have I allowed His joy to become my strength?

Once you discover the significance planted in the heart of your crisis, you will claim and live in a perpetual peace and spiritual rest. This is one of the hallmarks of God's Elect Ladies.

Many of them *know* they will never see the fruit of some of the things He elected them to do on this side of heaven. Yet they rejoice, trusting that they have laid a firm foundation by faith for those who will enter heaven's gates behind them.

Chapter 6

Don't Get Stuck in Transition

Throughout the Old West, from Kansas to California and from Texas to Oregon, you see the remains if you look for them. Old, rusted wagon wheel rims, the bleached bones of horses and cattle, and even discarded possessions and other lingering signs of humans long dead and forgotten.

Thousands of people dared to cross from the known into the unknown in search of a better life or for the fool's gold of instant riches during the Gold Rush era. Many of them never made it.

Some died in sudden snowstorms in high mountain passes; others died in flash floods, battles with Indians or other gold hunters, or in the searing heat of a desert crossing.

On the other hand, the people who were already there—the Native American tribes who had lived in the "unknown" areas for centuries—were faced with a transition of their own.

They had never faced a challenge on such a scale—all of their traditions and patterns of life were challenged. Some fought back, some moved on, and others did their best to adapt and accommodate what seemed to be inevitable.

There were many people on both sides who "got stuck in transition" and never reached the other side.

When you look at your circumstances and the situations that seem to be the source of your pain, it is easy to start judging yourself by the decisions you made or refused to make.

"I shouldn't have done that! And I should have *never* married that person. I should have slowed down, and I should have done this."

One of the worst things we can do in life is to beat up ourselves over decisions we've made that cannot be changed. It is useless to agonize about circumstances or events over which we now have no control. If you have repented of past sins, they are covered with the blood of Jesus. God does not remember them anymore, and neither should you.

You waste time and precious energy talking about or obsessively reliving all of the mistakes you've made, or recounting all of the painful things you've gone through. If you found yourself somehow stuck in a pit, would you spend your time staring at the bottom of the pit while wringing your hands and shaking your head? No! The way out is up, not down!

Your life isn't over, so you really need to look around and focus on what is *still there*, not on what is gone or stolen. This is especially true for an Elect Lady of God. Many of the special women who find themselves in this difficult place of election have no one to talk with, and even if they do have confidants, very few will truly understand their situations. They may—intentionally or unintentionally—serve to keep them in their crises.

It is a tragedy that there are so few people speaking to women who are in transition. We should be thankful for the few who do, because the Elect Ladies who catch hold of the vision of God experience life-changing transformation in their thinking, in their spirits, and in the way they live. It changes even the way they "talk to themselves," for example:

> *The vision of God brings life-changing transformation.*

I might not have a "headline" life worthy of star treatment and full-color spreads in the newspaper, the gossip sheets, or the best glamour magazines. I may not amount to much according to the rich and famous, but when I leave here, *I will make a mark in the earth* that will live from generation to generation.

Why? It is because God entrusted me with children. And I am giving my life to raise them—no matter what happens in this life. God trusted me with something that I didn't think I could be trusted with. I didn't think that I could even carry myself to the finish line, but God whispered something to me that was so far-fetched, and so far from my desire, that it seemed impossible. *But He told me I could do it!*

It seems to me that one of the most discouraging things in life, especially for women, is the *timing* of things. When we finally do perceive the call of God on our lives, it is often at our lowest point in life. We are still suffering from the crushing weight of personal grief.

Elect Ladies may feel they've lost all of their dreams, or they may wrestle with the nagging feeling that they never really achieved what they wanted in life. They haven't even won that inward battle before they begin to hear or sense something from God about their election. Even as they feel they are sinking, He calls them to stand strong in a lifelong struggle *for others*. (If it were easy, then there would be no "election" involved.)

Many years ago when I was a newly divorced single parent, the first thing I had to do was go through a grieving process. The circumstances of my life forced me to face the reality that I would never have what I thought I really wanted in life—because divorce was never part of that picture.

My plan was to live out my life with my original family in unbroken relationship and progression in the ministry. No normal person enters into marriage with divorce on his or her mind. Yet divorce did force its way into my life, and it changed everything. I did recover from my deep disappointment, but it took time, mercy, and a lot of grace.

I am convinced it is even *more* difficult and painful for Elect Ladies.

There comes a time when adverse circumstances and unhappy events push God's elect women to a "garden of Gethsemane experience" similar to what Jesus endured. They reach the point where they agonize over the choices common to a calling to any divine election:

Whose will wins out?

Will I choose to pursue my own will and my preconceived desires for my life? Or, will I say to God, "Not my will, but Yours, be done"?[1]

The "Gethsemane experience" is nothing less than a crushing, lonely place; a place of painful rejection, misunderstanding, and brokenness. It is rough enough to find yourself alone with God in such a heart-wrenching place of pain and sacrifice, but it can feel unbearable when no one wants to come along with you.

> "I'm in a transition; it's a hard place in my life that I just can't explain right now. Will you pray anyway? Will you cover me?"

When you've been in a place where you have cried until you can't cry anymore, it hurts to come back to the few friends or family members who dared to stay with you, only to find them *too sleepy, distracted, discouraged, and afraid* to pass the test with you. (See Matthew 26:36–45.)

Things get worse quickly when the few who remained at your side the longest finally pull you aside one day to say, "Well, you're really not what we thought you were going to be. To be honest, right now, we're really not interested in where you are going or who you are becoming. We're going in another direction—one that isn't quite so hard or lonely."

When God speaks to us, it is natural for us to look for confirmation and affirmation from the people closest and most important to us. We eagerly search for an "amen" or any word of encouragement to reassure us that somebody—anybody—might believe in the destiny planted in us!

It can be devastating to discover that no one understands or even wants to understand what is happening in our lives.

Most of the time, the kindest responses we get are comments more concerned with our own selfish well-being than with God's greater purposes in our situations.

> "Yeah, I hear you…but can't you just leave the children somewhere else, like with a family member someplace? How can you do it alone?"

> "Now why are you going through all that? Is it really worth it? What about you? Just cut off everything and everybody from the past and get a fresh start by yourself—without all those responsibilities and hassles. Those kids are just a ball and chain holding you down. In a few years, they won't even give you the time of day anyway."

> "Why are you staying in that marriage? He's just a jerk and you know it. Why fool yourself—you're not happy and he'll never change. The kids will work through it—they'll be fine with him. Just break free and take care of number one for a change."

Sometimes God calls a woman to stay in a painful and unhappy marriage. (I am *not* talking about women who face physical abuse, violence, or other life-threatening situations.)

There are many situations where a woman feels trapped in a marriage, and her life has nothing in common with the "happy Huxtable family" or with "Ozzie and Harriet."[2]

Perhaps you find yourself in a situation similar to what my mother faced many years ago, where you know it will be worse for the children if you leave than if you stay. There isn't anything in the marriage that really nurtures you, but you realize that if you pulled yourself out of the mess to find relief for yourself, you would also be withdrawing the spiritual covering of the house (because you are the Christian believer in the marriage).

Many of the folks who get stuck in this type of transition become entangled because most of the time they sit back and let life choose for them rather than making choices based on the understanding that they have been elected by God for a divine purpose.

I'm convinced there is a longing implanted deep inside every man and woman. It is the motivation behind their constant search for the reason or purpose behind their existence. Once they find it through the work of Christ, they can say, "This is what I've been sent to do."

We often see this universal longing of the heart surface in conversations. I've seen it show up repeatedly on television talk shows such as *Oprah* and others. The guests find themselves in spiritual discussions (whether "informed" or not), and it becomes

You've been sent to do the work of Christ.

clear that everyone in the conversation is searching for spiritual significance and meaning. One way or another, we are all running after the same thing.

Once you understand the *end* goal of the sacrifice in your life, a joy rushes in that supplies strength, endurance, and focus to take you through everything that comes along. How do I know? I take my cue from Jesus Christ. The apostle Paul explained it this way:

> *Let us run with endurance the race that is set before us, fixing our eyes on Jesus, the author and perfecter of faith, **who for the joy set before Him endured the cross**, despising the*

*shame, and has sat down at the right hand of the throne of
God.*   (Hebrews 12:1–2 NASB, emphasis added)

If you are an Elect Lady, then I'm writing this book for
you, and for anyone else—male or female, young or old—
who is being brought to the point of decision. Perhaps you've
already made the all-important decision to surrender your life
to Christ and follow Him. This is *another* decision, the one
you've been avoiding for a long time. This is the decision to
accept your election to an impossible task.

You will have to lay down the excuses, the "what if's," and
most of your "Why?" questions.

Can I just get you to say "yes" to God? There is a grace that
comes to you in the moment of surrender that will carry you
through your garden of Gethsemane and all the way through
the sacrifice to which you are called.

God is waiting to supernaturally work a miracle through
you and for you; and He always brings with it a peace that sur-
passes all understanding and comprehension. And He prom-
ises to guard your mind and protect your heart all the way
through. (See Philippians 4:6–7.)

The impossible task you are called to might take out a
thousand on your left, and ten thousand on your right—but
when God elects you to do a job, you will succeed where everyone else who tries it apart from divine calling is doomed to
fail. (See Psalm 91:7.)

Perhaps you have been going for years with a "no" in your
mind. If your heart has changed to "yes," then a joy is filling
you right now. Let me assure you that regardless of what comes
tomorrow or next year, your outward circumstances can never
steal your joy.

The path of "yes" to God's election is the same path that carried Jesus all the way from the cross to the grave, and beyond the resurrection to the right hand of the Father. It is the *right* path for you.

If you have already passed this point, and you said "yes" to the Lord long ago, you may be wondering why you should go any further with this book. It is because *most of the people you run into each day have broken dreams.*

What will you say to people who carry the pain and scars of disappointment created when the things they hoped for when they were in college or during a younger period did not come to pass? They thought life would be one way, but all of a sudden their dreams were shattered. Now they live fractured lives, carrying the dull ache of undiscovered purpose deep inside their hearts.

When your paths cross, do you believe it is an accident or a divine appointment? (I think you already know my answer to the question.)

Are you prepared to help someone who asks you in tears, "What do you do when your life shatters in front of your eyes? What do you do when your plans, your dreams, and everything that you were told when you were young becomes a mere fairy tale destined to never come true?"

Whether you are male or female, your life isn't your own. You and I have been *"bought with a price"* (1 Corinthians 6:20; 7:23 NASB). We have been set free to live for Jesus and bring freedom to others in His name.

When these people come to you, it is your opportunity to say, "I am not where I thought I would be, but I am where God wants me to be." You can encourage them to find His destiny for their lives here on earth.

In contrast, too many of us "saved and sanctified church people" adopt a mentality that says, "I want to see into heaven. Things will be great once we get there." If you ask me, I think God tells us the perspective He wants us to take in Revelation 4:1 (NASB). That is where He says, *"Come up here, and I will show you what must take place after these things."*

God doesn't want us to look *into* heaven; He wants us to look at things *from* heaven.

The only way to properly understand or perceive God's will in the midst of your shattered dreams and to come to grips with them is to see your destiny and what you were elected to do *from the position of God's high place.*

God wants us to look at things from heaven.

If you're saved, I say, "See it from heaven." When you board an airplane and look down from a great height, those big houses, shopping centers, and skyscrapers aren't that big anymore. Every large space suddenly seems smaller because you are seeing it from a higher perspective.

One time I took a flight out of Charlotte, North Carolina, during a thunderstorm. The ride was very rough during takeoff because we had to pass through some major cloud formations. About twenty minutes later, the entire scene was transformed in such a dramatic way that it still sticks out in my memory. We topped out over the cloud layer and were washed in brilliant sunlight! Obviously, everything looked different to us than it did when we were under the influence of the storm.

When I was on the ground, all I could see were dark storm clouds, driving rain, wind, and lightning flashes. Everywhere you looked, people were huddled under cover for protection from the fury of the storm, and the sun was nowhere to be found.

The illusion that the sun had disappeared wasn't real—it was still shining. The earth was still spinning in its precise orbit around its solar center. So what changed between the time I boarded the plane during the thunderstorm and the moment we were bathed in sunlight? We had been lifted to a new, higher perspective.

We have a whole generation and a culture that needs to be lifted to a new, higher perspective. We constantly seem to battle depression (or are constantly running and scheming to avoid it) because things just haven't gone the way we want them to go.

As if our own personal disappointments aren't enough to deal with, we have developed an entire media environment of books, magazines, and feature television shows displaying the spectacular successes of a few people as if that is what we should all be enjoying.

We begin to compare our disappointing lives with that of Bill Gates or some other famous and wealthy celebrity. Then some of us go a step further and imagine that it works for everybody else *except* for us, and resign ourselves to our inevitable fate: "Now I'm stuck in life with no hope."

A growing number of Americans are beginning to evaluate life—perhaps for the first time because a large segment of the population is getting older now. People entering their early forties to early sixties are beginning to think, "Oh, now my life is nearly over." In reality, it is just beginning.

I am in my fifties, and for the last ten years, I've been telling my congregation, "I just figured out what life is about.

But as one man said, 'Youth is a gift; unfortunately, when you recognize that, you're too old to enjoy it.'"

It seems to me that our nation recently completed a forty-year generational cycle. One of the Greek terms for generation is *dore* (pronounced "door"), which means "a revolution of time, an age or generation." More and more people are beginning to realize they've been pursuing the wrong things—and they're looking for the things that really matter. Unfortunately, they're launching the search loaded down with a lot of brokenness and disappointment.

I don't think many wide-eyed teens or optimistic "twenty-somethings" can accurately predict where they will be or what they will be doing at the age of forty or fifty.

Many folks, both men and women, are entering their middle-aged period with a string of broken relationships haunting them. They have children in two or more places, allotted to ex-spouses or partners in multiple cities.

Some are reaching their peak in knowledge, experience, or ability, but their jobs are becoming obsolete or are being farmed out to foreign suppliers. They may be forced out by companies trying to ditch their retirement fund responsibilities while looking for the cheapest workers.

What is life all about? You may be older now, with mandatory or early retirement staring you in the face. You followed all the rules, you showed up to work early and went home late, and your company is trying to cheat you out of your retirement or is facing hostile assimilation into another company.

Grandparents about to enter retirement are taking on parenting responsibilities around the country because their grown sons and daughters drop or fail in their responsibilities to raise their own children. Many of God's Elect Ladies fall into this category of weary and hope-worn caregivers.

I suspect that God has even moved aside some people so that godly grandmothers could impart kingdom principles to their grandchildren. If you are one of God's Elect Ladies raising your children's children, then you probably thought life would be easy—only to suddenly find yourself laboring and praying day after day to raise your grandchildren as you go deeper and deeper into your senior years.

Don't get stuck in transition. Honestly, I don't think most people really want to stay there, but they don't know how to break through to the victory. God's anointing and provision are upon you—trust Him and stay faithful one day at a time. If you follow the steps that God has given you for today, and trust Him to lead

You can leave a godly mark that will affect generations.

you once again tomorrow, you will discover the great things He is preparing for you and will leave a godly mark in the land that will affect generations after you until the Lord returns!

ENDNOTES

1. See Luke 22:42, where Jesus experienced this battle of wills between His spirit and His body and soul, which were longing to live.

2. The "Huxtables" were the fictitious 1980s TV sitcom family created by Bill Cosby, who came to represent the ideal upscale African-American family—an ideal that is rarely seen in real life. The same is true of Ozzie and Harriet Nelson, a

mild-mannered, real-life husband and wife team whose family was portrayed on an early television program and came to symbolize the "ideal" American family for several generations.

Chapter 7

How to Keep Going after Saying "Yes"

O nce you say "yes" to God in any area (whether you are male or female), you will have to say "no" to some of your friends and family and to the critics who refuse to accept your election.

Jesus even had to say "no" to His mother, brothers, and neighbors when they failed to perceive a change in His calling and earthly function. Jesus was no longer merely the Son who had grown up in Nazareth. The time had come for this Son Mary had covered to rise up and cover the world on behalf of His heavenly Father. (See John 7:1–8; Matthew 12:46–50; 13:54–58.)

This message to God's Elect Ladies can really light a fire under some of the old-line church government folks. When I examine the Scriptures, I see that while Jesus was still on the cross, He gave Mary authority to cover John as a mother, just as clearly as He asked John to cover Mary as his own mother.

Yet, even the idea of calling Mary or any other woman "elect" to a divine calling will upset some of the top-heavy religious "apple carts" blocking free entrance into service in God's House today. Jesus has been known to upset religious vendor carts before; it appears He is at it again. (See, for example, Matthew 21:12–16; Mark 11:15–18.) I didn't pick this fight—God did.

So whenever I get the chance, I warn people in the kingdom of God (men in particular) to change some of their non-biblical thinking. Every opinion must conform to the "whole counsel of God" rather than to a few out-of-context passages that favor some private interpretation of Scripture.[1]

No longer will men get away with looking at women as second-class individuals possessing secondary or lower priority gifts. This Bible truth is forcing me to upset and challenge some traditional religious windmills, but the fact of the matter is that God doesn't view women as "Grade B" material for leadership or ministry!

Frankly, if it comes to offending someone for the sake of God's Word, it just doesn't bother me. That is good for everyone because it encourages us to examine the Scriptures to understand why we think what we think!

One of the most serious challenges in the body of Christ is our habit of "tabernacling" or camping around yesterday's ways without ever really questioning or reviewing them *in the light of God's Word* and the *direction of the Holy Spirit.*[2]

THE EMPTY ANSWER WE DREAD: "OH, THAT'S HOW WE'VE ALWAYS DONE IT"

Too often, we discover we have become degraded copies of copies. The bottom line is this: Will we find ourselves embarrassed by our response to the question, "Why do you do it like that?" Above all, I dread giving someone the empty answer, "Oh, that's how we've always done it." The right response is, "Let's open the Bible and really look at it."

When Jesus and the apostles walked the earth, they preached and declared "the kingdom of God" rather than the local synagogue or Israel. The kingdom spans the generations and includes the total mystery of God's plan for man from before the beginning of time to beyond the end of time to eternity.

The cross, the blood, and the principles of new covenant life are eternal kingdom truths by which every local church should be governed, regardless of denominational or nondenominational backgrounds or historical settings.

I belong to the kingdom of God, so I am a kingdom man governed by the kingdom principles presented in God's Word. Therefore, I don't look at people as Jews or Greeks, as male or female, or as slaves or free. For example, we have transcended gender because God's Word says His kingdom transcends gender in Galatians 3:28. That means that if you have not transcended gender discrimination, then you will definitely have a problem with God's message about some of His Elect Ladies whom He's calling to lead.

Certain people will be offended by this book. I had to face that reality when trying to decide whether or not to write it. It wasn't a difficult decision. Long ago, I decided to stand on what God says in His Word rather than dance in step with the claims of critics or the ever-shifting whims of popular culture.

KINGDOM TRUTHS OFFEND THE RELIGIOUS MORE THAN THE SECULAR!

What amazes me is that kingdom teachings like this one offend some of my most "tradition-bound" opponents because of their *religious* traditions *even more* than they offend "politically correct" secular critics holding political or cultural opinions directly opposed to God's kingdom.

This is an important guideline in studying God's Word for guidance in life: If in doubt, go back to the original intent of God as described in the beginning.

The book of Genesis tells us God created the human race, male and female. He *empowered us* to rule His creation together. (See Genesis 1:26–28.) From the very beginning of our species, God created men and women to be equal in essence and different in function.

Why are we so absolutely determined to add to the Word of God, thinking we can improve upon His perfection with our limited thinking?

Some men still expect women to walk ten paces behind them and occupy the place of the "fallen half of the race," when in *real life,* women are covering their children throughout this broken society! Many can't submit to their husbands because the men are often *absent without leave;* and many of the men who are "there" actually endanger everyone close to them.

ABIDE IN THE VINE

I thank God for every woman with the courage and character to cover her children and raise them in an environment of self-sacrifice and faithful love. I commend single parents who have agreed to stay in a difficult situation just to receive and hold on to the treasure God placed in their care.

Have you read what Jesus said about "abiding in the vine"?

> *Abide in Me, and I in you. As the branch cannot bear fruit of itself, unless it abides in the vine, so neither can you, unless you abide in Me. I am the vine, you are the branches; he who abides in Me, and I in him, he bears much fruit; for apart from Me you can do nothing.* (John 15:4–5 NASB)

Let me boil down what I think is the essence of what Jesus is saying to you in this passage:

Your joy and power are in what I've elected you to do.

What happens when you step into alignment, when you say "yes" to God's election? All of God's resources, with all of His grace and mercy, become available to you from that point on. I am *not* saying everything gets better instantly, but it is true that *you* get better immediately.

Each time you say "yes" to God, another part of your life and will comes into *alignment* with God's purpose for your life. According to God's Word, He has deposited heavenly treasure in earthen vessels (see 2 Corinthians 4:7)—in other words, God has deposited a treasure in all of us. The life of Christ in us enables us to fulfill His good purposes for us as we yield to Him.

When we talk about alignment, the first thing that comes to my mind is the dial of a safe. The only legitimate way to open up a safe is to spin the combination dial in the right sequence of numbers. Each time you come to the correct number in the correct order (moving clockwise and counterclockwise and sometimes spinning all the way around the dial two times or more), then a tumbler drops in. This clears you to go to the next step in the process of reaching and accessing the treasure within.

Likewise, as you go through the trials and triumphs of life, you drop something here and see something released there. Then your life takes an unexpected spin, and you seem to land in another situation requiring patient persistence until a "tumbler" drops. In time, we begin to understand that we are being placed into alignment for a release of God's best for our lives.

I experienced a moment of unplanned awe in my life the moment I grabbed my mother and begged her, "Don't go!" A "tumbler" dropped that released God's life-changing grace into my situation.

When my school counselor grabbed me during my senior year, pulled me into the office, and spoke the truth to me about my potential and the importance of attending college, yet another "tumbler" dropped into the God-ordained combination of my life.

Almost immediately after Mary said "yes" to God, life became even more difficult. But His grace and mercy filled her life and helped her persevere. Now that you've said "yes," how will you keep going?

SAYING "YES" EMPOWERS YOU FOR THE JOURNEY

Have you ever really thought about Mary's situation from her viewpoint? As I previously mentioned, she never expected Joseph to die young. I just can't believe that Joseph's premature death was a part of her dreams about life and raising a family.

Even after you say "yes," bad things still happen sometimes. You still get those unexpected life interruptions that seem to totally rewrite the direction of your life. The obedience of saying "yes" doesn't necessarily make the road easier, but it *does* allow God to empower you for the journey.

Jesus was rejected by His own even though He made *all* the right choices and lived a sinless life. His choices (His obedience) didn't allow Him to escape persecution or opposition, but they empowered Him to perceive and seize the joy awaiting Him when all things were complete. (See Hebrews 5:8–9; 12:1–13 for a clear picture of the roles played by obedience and joy on the path of election.)

Do you realize that *your obedience* to God's election may release a whole new dimension of grace, mercy, and peace in the lives of *others*?

> *Your obedience releases grace in the lives of others.*

You, too, can tap the strength found in joy by understanding what your sacrifice will do for *others* in the days and years to come. Salvation, hope, and a future may come to many tomorrow because you were willing to say "yes" to the will of God today.

Now keep in mind the fact that peace—by biblical definition and demonstration—has never meant "the absence of trouble." It means God's stability in the midst of any and every kind of storm we encounter in life.

Mark's gospel gives us a perfect picture of *peace* in its description of the day Jesus and the disciples were caught in a small fishing boat during a storm. Some of the disciples on that ship had been professional fishermen before they dropped everything to follow Jesus.

They Knew the Lake and the Storm— But They Didn't Know Jesus

We know the storm was a bad one because those men were "locals" who grew up fishing on that lake. They were convinced they were going to die because they knew all about the storms that funneled down onto the lake, along with all of their dangers. The problem is that they didn't know enough about *Jesus*.

We think we know the ways of life, and we know all about the storms overtaking our lives; but do we know Jesus well enough? The amazing thing about this account is that when Jesus finally woke up and found His disciples paralyzed in terror, He simply said, *"Peace, be still!"* and the storm stopped raging. (See Mark 4:36–41.)

Jesus and the disciples were *already in peace* because the Bible says Jesus *"is our peace"* in Ephesians 2:14. A new perspective came to me when I looked at this incident from the fresh perspective that Jesus simply told the chaos to stop and peace to reign.

Even at the height of the storm—when the ship was rocking from side to side and the disciples were desperately rowing for the shore—all of them were enveloped in the peace of God. His peace is perpetual and continuous. But it seems as if Jesus' command effectively caused peace to manifest "in the *now*"—in the natural elements as well as in the spiritual realm. Compare the way a still photograph illustrates something in a totally different way from how we might see it in a motion picture or a television show. When the storm rages around us, it's hard to see, but when Jesus says, "Peace, be still," it's as though everything stops and you can see the way He has created to get you out of the situation.

Afterward, Jesus rebuked the disciples, saying essentially, "Look, you should be able to handle this! What happened to your faith?" (See Mark 4:40.)

WE DOUBT HE CARES WHEN WE THINK WE ARE DROWNING

Our passage through life is much like the disciples' attempt to pass to the other side of the Sea of Galilee. The winds of change and adversity rock us from one extreme to another, making us doubt whether the One who is in the boat with us really cares that we are "drowning."

We deal with anger one day and apathy the next; and the following day might bring us face-to-face with arrogance, pride, depression, or low self-esteem. We're tempted to believe that our problems are bigger than the God inside of us.

The apostle Paul put it this way, and then gave us the solution to it all:

> *I don't understand myself at all, for I really want to do what is right, but I don't do it. Instead, I do the very thing I hate....It seems to be a fact of life that when I want to do right, I inevitably do what is wrong....Who will free me from this life that is dominated by sin? Thank God! The answer is Jesus Christ our Lord....So now there is no condemnation for those who belong to Christ Jesus.*
> (Romans 7:15, 21, 24–8:1 NLT)

Each of us becomes more like Jesus through a *process*, a mostly forward movement marked in gradual steps of obedience, learning, adjustment, and humility before God and with His help.

HELP, GOD! I'M SLIPPING BACKWARD...

At times, you may feel as if you are slipping backward almost as much as you are moving forward! This is especially true for God's Elect Ladies, who so often must endure this process alone, without a support network of caring Christian friends and peers who understand their situation.

To make things even more difficult, most of the people around them just don't understand why they won't lower their standards enough to "get a man" at any cost. They can't understand why they won't ship the kids off to somebody else and go party with their friends. Again, sometimes you have to say "no" after you say "yes."

God will never let you sink or drown.

We want everything to become as still as it was for the disciples that day on the sea. However, right now, on *this* side of heaven, things aren't going to be "still" for us just because we want it to be so. The Lord wants us to learn how to stay in peace even in the middle of a raging storm. If you can discover and remember *who He really is* and understand that He is with you in every situation, then you will know He will never let you sink or drown! The prophet Isaiah revealed this secret to staying in peace:

> *Thou wilt keep him in perfect peace, whose mind is stayed on thee: because he trusteth in thee. Trust ye in the LORD for ever: for in the LORD JEHOVAH is everlasting strength.*
>
> (Isaiah 26:3–4 KJV)

IN CHRIST, YOU CAN RISE TO THE TOP EVERY TIME

When God is at the center of your life, you have supernatural "buoyancy," an ability to rise to the top in every situation, which defies explanation. God places something in you by His Spirit that makes it impossible for you to drown. How can I make such a claim? It isn't me; it was the apostle Paul who said,

> *No temptation has overtaken you but such as is common to man; and God is faithful, who will not allow you to be tempted beyond what you are able, but with the temptation will provide the way of escape also, that you may be able to endure it.* (1 Corinthians 10:13 NASB)

You might get bounced around and turned upside down sometimes, but you will never stay down or go under! It is impossible when you live in the resurrection of Jesus Christ.

Keep your mind fixed on Jesus and His peace will carry you through.

Something about His presence keeps you afloat in every situation. Take courage—as long as you follow Him, God won't let you die until it's time for you to be reunited with Him. Through His mercy, grace, and peace, you will be able to stand and declare, "It's going to be tough, but I shall accomplish what I'm supposed to accomplish, and I'm empowered to finish what God began in me!"

I am convinced that we all come to a dark moment in life—even after saying "yes" to God—when we don't know what will happen next. We don't know if we will see another day or if we will lose the house. We don't know how things will play out or

103

when it will all end—but if we keep our hearts and minds fixed on Jesus, His peace will cover us and carry us through it all.

I DON'T KNOW THE FINAL OUTCOME, BUT I HAVE PEACE!

We will be able to say with authority and conviction, "At least I'm sure that I'm on the right road! I'm doing the right thing. Even though I don't know the final outcome for my situation today, I have peace because I know I am where I'm supposed to be!"

(I've told my congregation often that nearly every time I think I've "figured out" what God is going to do, I can strike it *off* the list of things He *will* do. Frankly, if you or I can figure it out, then it is highly unlikely the almighty God will ever go in that direction.)

Mary's life adventure began the moment she said, "Here am I, Lord." (See Luke 1:38.) She could not name or describe what was happening to her because it was new. She couldn't bottle it, package it, or put it in a book because the book was still being written through her life.

New chapters of the mystery of God unfolded in her life constantly, so she had to live in an attitude of "yes" to God, being totally dependent on His grace and mercy.

Once Mary said "yes" to God and His work in her womb became more and more noticeable, she had to say "no" to many of her family members and friends. She also had to go away for a time.

Mary gave up being the Mary she had dreamed of being most of her life. From the first morning of her divine pregnancy to her last breath on earth, Mary had to get up every morning as the mother of this miraculous Child.

HER IDENTITY CHANGED WITH A WORD

God changed Mary's identity with a word. He elected her to carry the Messiah long before the Messiah called the Twelve from their ships and other occupations. In one brief visitation when Mary said "yes," she went from being a young virgin daughter in her father's house to an outcast among men and an earthly "covering" over the Seed of God, Jesus.

When you don't fully know what to do in the election of God, you do what you *do* know to do. It is there, on the precipice of faith and obedience, that God provides mercy, grace, and peace. Paul described this place to the Ephesians:

> *Therefore, take up the full armor of God, that you may be able to resist in the evil day, **and having done everything** [that you know to do], **to stand firm.***
> (Ephesians 6:13 NASB, emphasis added)

If you have no peace, you may be trying to fit your life and calling into the accepted group norm. Understand that the move and election of God will usually pull you *out* of the crowd and outside of accepted and "normal" boundaries.

GOD'S ELECTION MAKES EXPERTS OBSOLETE

The election of God can actually make experts obsolete, because although they know what has worked in the past, they don't always know the power of God. It can also cause you to become especially sensitive with spiritual discernment regarding your calling. It produces the daring boldness you need to embrace "outside-of-the-box" thinking. Again, it was Paul who wrote,

> *For consider your calling, brethren, that there were not many wise according to the flesh, not many mighty, not many noble;*

but God has chosen the foolish things of the world to shame the wise, and God has chosen the weak things of the world to shame the things which are strong,...that no man should boast before God. (1 Corinthians 1:26–27, 29 NASB)

Too many of us live like trained circus elephants, spending our lives tied down by a ridiculously tiny rope anchored by a puny stake in the ground and performing to please people. How do you get a wild animal weighing several tons to live in such captivity? It starts when it is young and small.

The trainer ties a rope around a young elephant's leg and anchors it to a stake driven about two or three feet into the ground. As the elephant grows, it never dawns on him that even a very small tug on that rope from his massive body would quickly uproot the stake or snap the rope or chain.

> *Saying "yes" to God changes the way you used to think.*

We're like those circus elephants when we get confined by our thoughts. We are locked into "the way it was" and "this happened to us last time we tried something new... years ago." Only God's anointing will snap the yoke of our slave mentality and launch us on a new life of divine freedom in Christ.

JUST SAY "NO" TO OLD THINKING

Therefore, once you say "yes" to God's election in your life, you have to say "no" to how you *used to think.* You must learn how to live in true freedom, and your love for Him is your guide!

Jesus loved His Father, and He was obedient to Him in every point. When the Bible tells us that Jesus endured the cross *"for the joy that was set before Him"* (Hebrews 12:2), we know that it was love that led Him to the cross. He loved His Father, and His Father had asked Him to lay down His life. He also loved the world, and although He who was Life had never known death, He saw something beyond the barrier of death that made Him willing to give up His life for it!

That same risk-taking spirit gets hold of us when we love our Savior and surrender all to Him. We may not know the "what" or the "how" of it all, but we know "Whom" we long to please and bless, so we have to do it.

The apostle Paul was willing to sacrifice everything he had trained for and valued the most—his education, his reputation, his Pharisaic commission from the Sanhedrin, and his very *life*—just because he had met the One, the Messiah, Jesus Christ.

Very few North American Christians are willing to entertain any form of "sacrifice" in their lives. We have weakened the body of Christ through our failure to present the gospel in such a way that people are willing to *die for it*.

I May Have to Die to Birth Life

Anyone who begins to understand the profound meaning and importance of God's election is forced to consider the thought, "I may have to die and give up my life to birth this thing into the kingdom."

Three of the gospels quote Jesus saying, "If any man would follow Me, let him deny himself and take up his cross." (See Matthew 16:24; Mark 8:34; Luke 9:23.) There is only one use for a cross—back then, they didn't use crosses to decorate churches or for personal decoration as jewelry.

What's the other side to this gospel? What is the thing that grounds us? Where are the heroes who die in their faith?

The old saints of fifty years ago seemed to understand suffering far better than we do. They went through nationwide economic depression, extreme prejudice, violence, and two World Wars that nearly destroyed Western civilization. Perhaps this is why "the old church" seemed to understand suffering and death better than we do.

This deep understanding even showed up in their favorite songs, including "The Old Rugged Cross" and "Nothing but the Blood." A lot of "me-centered" folks in the modern church scoff at those songs—but that is because they don't have understanding.

If you receive the election of God to a difficult or seemingly impossible task, then He will cause you to believe in and love something so much that you will begin to proclaim,

> It is for this cause I have come. I may not have the fancy house I used to dream about, but this passion in me won't let me settle for less than success.
>
> I have to bring this baby into the world. I have to see my sons and daughters rise up in strength, power, and holiness—no matter what is stacked against them. I refuse to surrender my grandbabies to the 'hood.
>
> Nobody is going to steal my family from me and God. I will cover with my life what God elected me to cover. They'll have to come through me first, and I'm not going down because God is holding me up!

When the election of God grips your heart, His passion isn't far behind. When you finally say "yes," then you've found something and Someone you are willing to risk everything for. Now you can endure the pain, the sacrifice, and even the misunderstanding of family and friends as long as you can see the dream for which you are sacrificing.

ENDNOTES

1. The apostle Paul declared to Christians who were struggling to stand in a religious environment divided by rigid and partial teachings of God's Word, *"For I have not shunned to declare to you the **whole counsel** of God"* (Acts 20:27, emphasis added). We cannot afford to "clip out" or "hide away as unimportant" certain passages of God's holy Word—whether they reveal truths about His present-day supernatural gifts in operation, or offer seemingly "controversial" truths about sexual conduct, church government, and the active roles of women in the new covenant church. (See also 2 Peter 1:20–21.)

2. I would never encourage someone to challenge traditions merely for the sake of challenging the status quo. The apostle Paul personally *praised* believers who took the initiative to take the things they had heard him and other leaders say and to *study the Scriptures for themselves* to make sure they were true and accurate. (See Acts 17:10–12). My aim is to lead people—both personally and corporately—back to the Scriptures (and away from man-made traditions) as their supreme guide in all matters.

Chapter 8

Don't Reject Your Election: Make Your Acceptance Speech

S ometimes we know what we're elected to do, but we don't want to do it. When you reject your election, you basically challenge God to change His will. It is better to accept the election of God and move forward.

I can still remember the night I watched the 2003 gubernatorial election results in California. It made the evening news across the country because, according to the will of the people, the winner was the well-known celebrity Arnold Schwarzenegger. When he learned that he had won the race, he stepped before a mass of microphones and made an acceptance speech.

It's time to settle something. Have you made *your* acceptance speech for God's election in your life? You may be one of the millions of people standing on the sidelines missing the power and authority God has given them. Most of them have missed their opportunities because *they want something else.*

Are you succumbing to the "I/O Factor" that robs destinies and destroys the dreams of entire generations and people groups? You know you are fighting God's election if you reject His will using two major words.

Instead of standing up and thanking those who helped you accept your election, you say instead, *"If only...."* This is the "I/O Factor."

> *There are two deadly words: "If only."*

These two words are deadly. They lock you into an eternity of regret. They doom you to a hopeless future of backward thinking and endless stormy waves of remorse and rising winds of bitterness.

If only I had married this one instead of...

If only I had gone this way instead of...

If only I had stayed home that night instead of...

If only I had stayed in the front seat instead of the back seat...

If only I had said no at the party instead of...

If only I had finished high school instead of...

If only I had stayed in church and out of the bars...

GOD GAVE YOU THREE POWERFUL GIFTS

You can't change the past, but it is entirely possible to change your present and affect your future. God has given us three powerful gifts to set us free from the thoughts of "what if" and "if only." The three things I mentioned in the previous chapter—grace, mercy, and peace—are from Him alone. (You can't buy them at Wal-Mart or Target, or purchase them on the Internet.)

Grace is kindness or favor given when you do not deserve it. Is it possible the reason so many of us feel miserable most of the time is that we have never accepted the grace of God's forgiveness—and election?

Do you catch yourself asking friends and your spouse, "Why am I so tired and stressed out?" Many times we are just bucking what God called us to do! Now don't get mad at me—especially if you're already mad at God because you aren't where you think you should be! I can guarantee that God has assigned you a place, but is it possible that you are kicking against His assignment? That can really hinder the flow of God's unmerited favor. *He* still loves you, but *your* ability to receive from Him drops to zero.

If you still hold out, God has yet another remedy: *mercy.* Mercy is when God helps you in a miserable situation—whether it was caused by disobedience or by something unrelated to a failure on your part. God says, "I'll intervene in your life with a miracle. I will have mercy on you when you don't even think I should or would! Because I love you, I will step into your miserable situation and have mercy on you."

Grace and mercy are complemented by God's gift of supernatural *peace.* I couldn't care less whether I have the money and car as long as I can lay my head down and sleep without my mind running wild and playing tricks on me. Even when you don't understand everything that God is doing, He will give you a peace that will guard your heart and mind! (See Philippians 4:7.)

GOD INTERRUPTED YOUR LIFE TO SAVE IT

This message is for "the *Elect* Lady." God interrupted your life to save it; but until you accept what you were called to be and to do, His grace or mercy will elude you, and His supernatural peace will be hard to find. God calls to us and is ready to rescue us, but we must *come* to Him and find our place in His plans to receive His blessings.

When you have favor with God, people just have to bless you. Every time you turn around, you will discover that God is blessing you. Even if you mess up, His mercy will fall upon you and lead you to repentance and forgiveness. God can fix your "stuff" as long as you are obedient. No matter what you are going through, you will lay your head down at home and rest—you will have an abundance of peace (and your tormentor *won't*)!

God is saying,

Once and for all, Elect Lady whom I love—(and this includes any children you may have)—your life has been interrupted so that I can put a little mercy, favor, and peace in it—*if you can accept what I elected you to do.*

God is looking for people who will say, "I'm not going to fight You anymore, Lord. I didn't get the dream man I expected....I didn't get my childhood dreams, but I need mercy and grace. I've got to get my peace back!"

113

Listen, this isn't limited to just the Elect Ladies. There are some miserable men who have not accepted who God called them to be before the foundation of the earth!

I RAN UNTIL GOD INTERRUPTED ME

I didn't *choose* to be a preacher. My daddy was a preacher, and the *last* thing I wanted to be was a preacher. I actually *ran* from it until God interrupted my life. I got fired from a dream job, and He wouldn't let me sleep at night.

I actually went out to buy wine (I never could drink before then), thinking I could drink myself to sleep. It still didn't work—all I did was sit up *drunk* all night, with a hangover in the morning as a bonus.

> *You can run from God's plan, but He'll follow you.*

God loved me so much in His severe mercy that He would not give me the grace I longed for. He withheld His peace until I began to listen to His voice.

I resisted as long as I could because I'd grown up in a preacher's home. If you had asked me about it at the time, I would have said, "I don't want to be a preacher because I don't want to die broke like my daddy, surrounded by a bunch of unthankful people."

I finally accepted God's election to pastor and began serving my first church as senior pastor, but I only said "yes" to God through a struggle.

I enrolled in the ITC Moorehouse School of Religion in Atlanta, and everybody there had high hopes of pastoring a church in Atlanta. Atlanta is the "Mecca," the jewel of Georgia, where everyone wanted a prominent pastorate.

God had other ideas for me. I ended up serving a rural church congregation of forty souls a full eighty miles from my doorstep. That congregation in Cedartown, Georgia, was wonderful, but no one had joined the church or been saved for a whole year.

I was preaching, driving 160 miles round-trip two or three times a week, plus working a full-time job. I'd gone through a divorce and was also trying to raise two boys as a single parent—it was a challenge.

MAKE A DECISION—100 PERCENT OR NOTHING

My first choice would have been full-time ministry, but I couldn't afford it and the church couldn't afford to support me either. After three years, the church finally started to grow, but I had to make a decision. I knew I wasn't putting 100 percent into God's assignment, and God required all or nothing.

Cedartown had several churches, and it seemed as if every pastor there had the same mentality that I did: "I'm just hanging around here until something better comes along. None of the pastors in this town stays very long, so why should I? We're all hoping to go to Atlanta to take a *real* church." That was the history of ministry in that town, and even the townspeople expected their pastors to come and then go on to "bigger and better things."

Weeping and broken before God, I said, "Lord, I am going to pastor this church as if You've assigned me to these people for the rest of my life!" Then I made a public commitment to the people from the pulpit. "From now on I will have regular office hours, I'll conduct a Bible study, and I'll stay in town all day on Sundays because I am your pastor. I am here to stay."

Then I started looking for a house so I could move there and be closer to the flock.

UNWILLING OBEDIENCE AND LIP SERVICE WON'T DO

That was very difficult for me because it forced me to come to grips with what I wanted versus what I had. Would I really say "yes" to God, or would I give Him a little nod of reluctant obedience plus some lip service?

From that point on, I stopped looking for "something better" in Atlanta. When I gave up that dream, a godly contentment and peace came over me. A supernatural grace and joy flooded my life, and I became faithful to what God had assigned me to do. If this is my life's work, then this is what I'm going to do!

It was very refreshing, and almost from that moment, the church began to grow. Within three years, that tiny rural church of forty had grown to nearly three hundred members, and that is tremendous growth for a rural area. At least part of the reason was that the people sensed security and stability. "He's really here to stay; he's really concerned about us and he's not looking past us, hoping to go somewhere bigger and better."

Then the day came when a friend called from Atlanta to say that the pastor at New Birth Missionary Baptist Church had left, and he asked me to minister there for a Sunday service. The pastoral search committee had a thick application form ready for me and invited me to fill it out if I wanted to be considered as a candidate for the pastorate. I just said, "No, I'm not going to fill that out."

I went back to my church in rural Georgia and said to the Lord, "God, if I'm supposed to be there, then You will do it. If not, then I'm going back to pastoring my church."

ARE YOU "UNDER ASSIGNMENT" OR "ON THE HUNT"?

Basically, I broke all their rules because I was not trying to become the pastor at New Birth. I had learned that there are blessings that come when you are a man under assignment instead of a man on the hunt. I didn't want to be anywhere that God didn't want me to be. Somehow, God just made it happen.

This is my point: My move to Atlanta was a divine reassignment because I wasn't seeking to move anywhere. I was content with my assignment and I loved the people at my first church.

I didn't want to be anywhere God didn't want me.

At first, I had wrestled with it greatly because I didn't like driving 160 miles every time I went there. I didn't like having to work a full-time job, or having to feed my kids on the road (they even had to do their homework in the car in those days). I got up early every morning to work at my job and still attend my seminary classes.

God gave me the grace, the peace, and the mercy to do it. Looking back on that period in my life, I don't see how I got it done! God moved on my behalf *after* I proved myself faithful to His election in my life.

When the leadership at New Birth asked me to come (even though they didn't have a phonebook-sized application on file), I faced one of the most difficult decisions I've ever made in my life. It was agonizing, and the decision almost ripped me apart emotionally because I had fallen in love with my people at Cedartown.

117

MY HEART WAS "GOD-WARD" THROUGH IT ALL

Once I knew that God wanted me to accept His new election, I did everything I could to make the transition smooth, blessed, and godly. I gave advance notice and provided the search committee with the name of an anointed man with a faithful ministry call whom I knew would carry on with the same heart I had. The process still broke my heart, but at least I knew my heart was "God-ward" through it all.

As it turned out, the leadership didn't follow my recommendation and chose a pastor using more "traditional" methods instead, with somewhat predictable results. At least I tried my best to help them. Over time, a good number of the original congregation started coming to Atlanta to attend New Birth Missionary Baptist every week.

Once you accept God's election in your life, it becomes an anchor of stability in times of instability. I ended up at New Birth only because God put me there, and I knew I was supposed to be there.

That inner "knowing" has carried me through the hard years of early growth and struggle. Now it is carrying me through the difficulties of the latest phase, when I'm seeing many of the young men and women I've trained and mentored over the years answering their own call to preach and pastor elsewhere. Now I'll have to train a whole new group of leaders for this exploding ministry.

You have to recognize and accept God's election to tap His reservoir of mercy, grace, and peace. At this point in my life, I've come too far to even turn around. I know I'm too close to something that is about to move; I have to just keep pushing to get to the other side. I am captivated and captured by my investment in God's election!

Answering God's call to pastor churches was just another step in my acceptance of an even more basic election in my life—an election very similar to the call faced by millions of "Elect Ladies" across the world.

CALLED TO BE A FATHER TO THE FATHERLESS

For years, I've been led by God to take fatherless young men under my wing. Others were at risk in life for one reason or another. Sometimes I even took them into my home and raised them as my own sons. I am called to be a father to the fatherless.

At times I've been moved by God to pay their way through college or to help them move into ministry in one way or another. It has been a lifelong path and I feel I'll pursue it until my life is over.

God elected me, and I will obey Him no matter what the cost.

It has brought me a lot of criticism over the years, for several reasons, but I refuse to turn my back on something God has elected me to do. Many of the young men I've trained and raised are grown and married with families. They've landed good jobs, and some have graduated from college; many have bought their own homes and entered the ministry.

Many people on the outside looking in have said, "What does he want? Why does Long do that?" They have questioned my motives over and over again, but the truth is that God elected me to reach out to the fatherless, and I will obey Him no matter the cost. Many of God's Elect Ladies face similar situations and criticisms. I encourage you to accept your election and to make your election speech loud and clear to all who will hear.

IS THERE SOMETHING I HAVE TO GIVE THEM?

I have to admit that I've had my share of serious discussions with God about my election. This calling to mentor young men was difficult for my wife to understand, but she kept at it. This election takes some unique forms at times. I can meet a young man—whether people label him a "good" boy or a "bad" boy—and immediately know if there is something I have to give him for success in life.

Very quickly I realized that God didn't primarily call me to help the good boys—He sent me to help the young men who are in trouble, the guys with a record and a bad attitude. My election is sure, though. If you give me some time, you'll find even the worst of them changing.

I have kids of my own, but my viewpoint is that every kid is my kid. I don't think Christians in America can afford to care only about their own kids and ignore the problems of everyone else out there.

My mom raised her family as a "community house" where a new face was always welcome at the table. That "community house" heart is still beating strong in me. God's love is constantly leading me to pull people in and cover them with a father's covering. It's draining at times, and sometimes it's very thankless, but there is a joy that comes at the end of the process. I've accepted God's election, and I can't help myself.

I think that is what will happen to you when you finally grab hold of the things God really intends for you to do. It isn't a "job"; it is a joy. It is God's purpose lived out in the flesh. That is what being a pastor is to me. I don't have to make myself do it. I have to make myself *stop*!

Yet, let me warn you: Once you make your election speech, your public "yes" will change your crowd!

"Yes" puts you in the arena of aloneness. Think about Mary, who became the mother of Jesus. She grew up just like everybody else, became betrothed to Joseph exactly as her parents planned it, and began to make wedding plans.

THE ELECT LADY APPEARED TO BE TOTALLY OUT OF ORDER

Suddenly Mary was elected by God and became pregnant, with no earthly explanation. This Elect Lady *appeared* to be totally out of order and on the wrong side of all the teaching she had heard. In my mind, Mary's neighborhood didn't know how to deal with her, and everybody was whispering about her, but no one was talking to her.

Once she got caught up in the divine calling, she lost all conversation with the people who used to populate her world. They still had the respectability and were still pursuing the Jewish dream. But Mary's dream had been permanently interrupted.

Then she had to explain to her fiancé why she was pregnant, and hope against hope that he would agree to accept her election, too. In His mercy, God arranged for Mary to get an "amen to her loneliness" by sending her to visit Elizabeth, who was having her own election celebration.

The Bible never says that Mary convinced Joseph about the nature of her pregnancy. But we are told that Joseph was obedient to the angel's declaration and accepted his *own election* with actions that amounted to a loud "yes." (See Matthew 1:18–25.)

Joseph's life was interrupted by God, too. Again, when he said "yes," he committed himself to a life of social and religious disgrace. Imagine what happened at the local "shepherd's club" when he returned to his usual spot a few years later as a husband *and* as the supposed father of a young boy, born out of town.

Perhaps there weren't very many people willing to talk to Joseph, either; after all, wasn't he a candidate for the town fool for receiving his pregnant fiancée and pretending everything was all right?

ALL I KNOW IS "GOD TOLD ME"

All Joseph knew was, "God told me." He had to go against a whole standard of rules and religious tradition to stand by Mary. It meant he would live a life of isolation, so he had to take his loneliness to God.

No one really likes to think about the price we may pay in our families and communities—or with our lives—for the election of God. The prophet Isaiah accepted his election to prophesy the coming of our Savior and a broad scenario of end-time events. If tradition is accurate, he was sawn in half for his uncompromising prophecies of righteousness before an unrighteous king. Jeremiah was a social outcast whose true prophecies

God's divine calling may involve a price.

and dire warnings were largely unheeded by the people of Israel. Hosea was instructed to marry an adulterous wife as an analogy of the Israelites' unfaithfulness toward God. It is not easy to speak God's message to a wicked society that does not want to hear His call to holiness.

Who can bear the burden of being a trailblazer or forerunner? For example, who would want to grow up in a high priest's family and then not receive his father's name? John the Baptist was born after God locked his father's voice and wouldn't let him speak. On the day of circumcision, someone tried to name him after his father, but his daddy finally spoke out to say the boy's name would be John.

How would you feel if you begged God for a son, and after you finally get one, God won't even let you pattern him after yourself in the ancient priestly profession? Instead, God sent John out into the desert, where he ate bugs and wild honey, wears animal skins (with the hair still attached), and says crazy things calculated to start a holy war with your coworkers!

"WHAT'S WITH THE CAMEL SKINS, SON?"

Your only son would literally have been in the priestly rotation to burn incense in the Holy Place. Instead he's out there wearing camel skins and dunking people in muddy water. "What's with the camel skins, son?"

Can you imagine the interruption of all your dreams for his life? Yet, the fruit of John the Baptist's election will last for eternity. He was the one human being elected from the entire human race to *"prepare the way of the LORD"* (Isaiah 40:3), and he fulfilled his calling with excellence. John's election is eternally linked with the election of Jesus to lay down His life for humanity.

Perhaps in a similar way, we see someone linked with Mary in her election of God. Remember, the book of 2 John begins and ends with "elect" ladies.

John began his letter with the words, *"The elder unto the elect lady and her children"* (v. 1 KJV). At the end of his letter,

John wrote, *"The children of thy elect sister greet thee"* (v. 13 KJV).

The last time we heard anything about Mary's sister was in John 19:25, where John said she was standing right beside Mary during her exchange with Jesus on the cross. This should speak volumes to us.

MARY'S SISTER WAS ALSO AN ELECT LADY

Do you suppose that Mary's sister was there at her side because she had altered her life just to cover her sister? I am convinced this faithful sister was also an *Elect Lady*, a called and anointed sister who sacrificed her comfort and reputation to identify with her elect sister and silently strengthen her through all of her difficult trials.

She joins many other examples of people in the Bible who embraced "God interruptions" of their lives, such as Joseph, the son of Jacob; Zacchaeus, the height-challenged chief tax collector; and Bartimaeus, the blind beggar.

I know what it is like to struggle with God's direction and life's dejection too. After nearly leaving the ministry following a painful divorce, I finally decided to accept my election and started all over again in Cedartown. Then, three years later, God interrupted my life again with a divine reassignment.

Now at my seventeen-year mark at New Birth Missionary Baptist Church, God has me serving as senior pastor of a 25,000-member church with a ministry campus valued at over $90 million (we've only developed a third of it). We have become the largest investor in the county, other than a nearby shopping mall built just a few years ago.

My calling takes me all over the world, and God has given me influence in state and national political circles, in serving as CEO of a corporation, and in ministering as mentor and bishop for pastors and ministers internationally.

ACCEPT YOUR ELECTION AND MAKE YOUR SPEECH!

Accept God's election and make your final acceptance speech. Then prepare for an exciting and sometimes stretching ride with destiny. The greater and more difficult your election (and remember that what God calls "great" and what man considers "great" are usually two different things), the more difficult it will be to find people who *understand* your situation and offer support. Just press on by remembering your election and recalling your acceptance speech.

God will mature you to work out the imperfections.

Paul told the Christians in Philippi to *"work out [their] own salvation with fear and trembling"* (Philippians 2:12). God's gift of salvation is free, and we receive it by faith. But once you step into God's kingdom, He launches you on a process of maturity to *"work out"* the imperfections in your life. You will also be "working out" the perfect will of God and the election that He planted deep within you.

I am a preacher; I was elected by God to do it at any cost. I tried to do other things because I didn't *want* to be a preacher. God kept working with me until I realized I had to work that out of me.

The Bible speaks of *"Christ in you, the hope of glory"* (Colossians 1:27). Not only is that living hope dwelling inside you, but it is also your elected task in this life to *bring that hope forth into your everyday life.* Only then will it transform and deliver others through the power of Christ.

We veer off the road every time we try to work from things God never put in us. That is why I hammer so long and hard on this truth: "Destiny chooses you; you don't choose destiny."

> *"For I know the plans that I have for you," declares the LORD, "plans for welfare* [good] *and not for calamity* [disaster] *to give you a future and a hope."*   (Jeremiah 29:11 NASB)

Whatever God put in you before you were formed in your mother's womb is the divine destiny He ordained to be worked out of you. (See Isaiah 44:2.)

> *Don't try to choose what has already been chosen!*

The Spirit of Christ is at work in you, providing the willpower and the real power to do His good pleasure (the "Eddie Long translation" of Philippians 2:13).

We spend too much time trying to choose what's already been chosen. We create most of our own heartbreak because we run around in our own man-made enthusiasm and energy. We try to work out something in His name that He never ordained to be worked out of us. It was never deposited in us in the first place. You can only give what you have received.

What has He deposited in you?

Once you discover and accept your election in Christ, once you deliver your acceptance speech and step into your destiny, the awe of God will fall on your life. You will discover what it feels like to be fulfilled because you will be doing what you were created to do, and nothing else will have that same appeal or satisfaction.

Once I discovered my election and accepted it, I knew that I knew I was doing what I was supposed to do. Now, I don't go to work each morning—I go to life! I go for the sheer joy of it, and it just so happens that I even get paid for it!

Chapter 9

Silent Pondering, Public Suffering, Eternal Glory

T he burden of a secret can seem unbearable sometimes, and no secret is as difficult to keep as a secret given by God.

Somehow, I don't think Mary ran to her girl-friends in giddy excitement with a flushed face to tell them, "God told me my heart would be pierced through with many sorrows. I can hardly wait!"

Mary entered married life under the strang-est set of circumstances ever faced by a woman on earth. She married Joseph in a "shotgun wedding" orchestrated by God. Then she had to live with this man almost as if he were a friendly stranger for nine long and lonely months as they struggled to stand together as social outcasts roped into a cosmic struggle.

She had married the man of her dreams (or at least her parents' dreams in that day of arranged marriages), but Mary still couldn't enjoy the excitement of sexual union or the intimacy of soul it fosters between husband and wife. This virgin woman was carrying the Seed of Another and everything and everyone else would have to accommodate her election.

Highly trained medical specialists *still* scratch their heads, and critics of Christianity still try to build their hopeless case over the impossibility of a virgin woman giving birth to a child—yet it happened nevertheless.

The day Mary said "yes" to God, He shared some secrets with her through the archangel. These were the "weighty" kind of secrets, divine mysteries that still baffle Jewish theologians to this day (because the key to these mysteries is the identity of Jesus Christ as the Messiah of the Scriptures). Even the "simple" words seemed to carry eternal weight.

Imagine a teenage Jewish girl hearing these words from Gabriel, one of the two great archangels who dwell in the very presence of God: *"Hail, favored one! The Lord is with you"* (Luke 1:28 NASB).

The next verse tells us Mary was *"greatly troubled"* by these words, and she *"kept pondering"* or questioning why Gabriel the archangel had greeted her the way he did. It is easy to understand why.

WHAT WAS SHE THINKING?

Look closely at what Gabriel told Mary (along with a few insertions of possible thoughts and "ponderings" that *might* have gone through her mind):

And the angel said to her, "Do not be afraid, Mary [It's too late for that…]; *for you have found favor with God.* [How could I have favor? I'm still surprised that He even knows my name…and what is favor?] *And behold, you will conceive in your womb* [Uh, what was that again?], *and bear a son, and you shall name Him Jesus. He will be great, and will be called the Son of the Most High* [Son of who? What about Joseph?]; *and the Lord God will give Him the throne of His father David* [My son will be royalty? Now I know Joseph is descended from King David's line, but I thought he wasn't involved in this… and how could my son take David's throne?]; *and He will reign over the house of Jacob forever; and His kingdom will have no end."* [How could my son's kingdom never end? Doesn't everybody die? Now, I suppose God knows what I've been thinking about as my marriage day comes closer—but I just can't figure all of this out.] *And Mary said to the angel, "How can this be, since I am a virgin?"* (Luke 1:30–34 NASB)

Mary received even more secrets to ponder as the days turned into months and years (and this is only a partial list).

1. She learned that her relative, Elizabeth, had become pregnant in her old age! Everybody said she was barren or infertile, but Gabriel revealed that Elizabeth was already in her sixth month! (See Luke 1:36.)

2. When Mary walked in to Elizabeth's house, something came over her and she suddenly grabbed her stomach and virtually shouted out her own surprise greeting to Mary, calling her *"blessed*

among women" and saying the *"fruit"* of Mary's womb was blessed. (See Luke 1:42.)

3. Then Elizabeth jumped all the way off the edge when she called Mary *"the mother of **my Lord**,"* and explained that her baby leapt for joy in her womb as soon as she heard Mary say hello! (See Luke 1:43–44, emphasis added.)

4. Mary herself began to praise the Lord under the inspiration of the Holy Spirit, using imagery from the Psalms, and the books of Job and Genesis. (See Luke 1:46–55.)

5. Shepherds tracked down Joseph and Mary in Bethlehem in the animal stable where Jesus had just been born. They said angels visited them that night in the fields, saying, *"a Savior, who is Christ the Lord"* (Luke 2:11 NASB) had been born in Bethlehem. The Bible says, *"And **all who heard it** [there were more there than just Mary and Joseph] wondered at the things which were told them by the shepherds. **But Mary treasured up all these things, pondering them in her heart"*** (Luke 2:18–19 NASB, emphasis added).

6. An aged, *"righteous and devout"* man (Luke 2:25) named Simeon entered the temple in Jerusalem eight days after Jesus' birth, when Mary and Joseph presented Jesus to God with an offering for Him as a firstborn son. He took Jesus in his arms and prayed to God, *"My eyes have seen Your salvation"* (v. 30).

7. After Simeon blessed the amazed parents, he prophesied directly to Mary: *"Behold, this Child is*

*appointed for the fall and rise of many in Israel, and for a sign to be opposed—**and a sword will pierce even your own soul**—to the end that thoughts from many hearts may be revealed"* (Luke 2:34–35 NASB, emphasis added).

8. Mary hadn't even recovered from Simeon's shocking prophecy when an eighty-four-year-old widow walked up who was known to everyone in Jerusalem as "the prophetess who fasts and prays night and day" in the temple. She took one look at Jesus and began to praise God out loud! She *kept* on praising Him, and Mary and Joseph heard that she kept speaking about Jesus to everyone who was serious about the Messiah who would redeem Jerusalem! (See Luke 2:36–38.)

9. After twelve relatively "normal" years, Mary was jolted back into the reality of her divine election when Jesus disappeared from the family traveling party while they were returning home after the annual Passover celebration in Jerusalem. When they found Him in the temple three days later, He said, *"Why is it that you were looking for Me? Did you not know that I had to be in My Father's house?"* (Luke 2:49 NASB). The Scriptures add, *"And they did not understand the statement which He had made to them"* (v. 50 NASB).

SET APART TO EMBRACE GOD'S WILL— "WHATEVER"

As I said before, Mary never expected Joseph to die so soon, and like any normal mother, she desperately hoped her children would all outlive her. Yet she was an Elect Lady, a woman set apart to embrace the will of God—"whatever."

She faced the unknown the only way any of us can face such things—by relying upon the Unchanging One. Mary also had to lean upon God's faithfulness to face the burden of what she *did* know.

She carried the burning memories of all those angelic revelations she'd heard, describing what would happen with her Son. How many times a day and how many nights did Mary lay awake pondering the meaning and dreading the fulfillment of the prophetic declaration, *"A sword will pierce even your own soul"*?

The woman who carried the Seed of God and gave birth to our Savior also carried a burden in her soul that remained with her all the days of her life. I strongly suspect that most of God's Elect Ladies, and even His Elect Men, have heard things or received revelations that they must carry in their hearts and ponder all of their days.

Mary determined to embrace the will of God.

It is time to address the silent ponderings and quiet reflections that take up residence in our hearts after God speaks divine secrets to us—those things that we can't talk about, the things that we wouldn't know how to share with other people even if they could handle them. These are often the things we live with and walk in, the things that may trouble us at times.

Most of us echo these words of Mary when we receive a genuine visitation from God: "How can this be?" His ways really *are* higher than our ways, and His thoughts are infinitely greater than our thoughts and powers of comprehension. (See Isaiah 55:9.)

The only way we can begin to comprehend God's ways is for Him to purposely simplify His words for us while enlarging our capacity to receive and understand.

I HEAR YOUR WORDS, BUT I CAN'T COMPREHEND YOUR WAYS

Mary heard the angel Gabriel's words, but she couldn't comprehend the ways in which God would work out the details. She couldn't figure out how such things could come to pass— even after the angel answered her question.

> *"How can this be, since I am a virgin?" And the angel answered and said to her, "The Holy Spirit will come upon you, and the power of the Most High will overshadow you; and for that reason the holy offspring shall be called the Son of God."* (Luke 1:34–35 NASB)

Mary accepted what the angel said and believed God, even though she didn't understand the process. Yet, when God reveals secrets about His plan for our lives, many of us begin to evaluate our worth. It is natural to wonder what made us so special that God elected us for a special purpose, but then we begin to seriously doubt that we are worthy enough to walk in what we heard. In other words, natural thinking can easily lead us into disobedience rooted in unbelief.

It is almost as if the Lord picks times, locations, and situations of life for us to experience that are the *opposite* of our destiny. This tests our faith when we are called. David was destined to be king over Israel, but God called him and prepared him in the sheep fields far from the silk sheets and royal trappings of a palace.

SOMETIMES YOU HAVE TO GO DOWN TO GO UP

If God says (as He did to Abraham), "I'm going to bless you, and your seed will be a blessing to a thousand generations, and you will be wealthy," then the word will probably come to you at your poorest moment. It will arrive after you've been childless and infertile for eighty years—and at a time when it looks like nothing is going to change! Sometimes you have to go down to go up, and you must give up everything to gain everything.

To make this point clear to my congregation recently, I placed three hundred dollars in cash on a chair near the pulpit. Then I told a young lady in the congregation, "That three hundred dollars in cash is your destiny." At the same time I grabbed her by the hand and started preaching.

Sometimes you must give up everything to gain everything.

I led that confused young lady through the congregation seated in the pews. I would stop and say, "We are over here right now, but that money is your destiny." Then I'd lead her to even more places that were farther away from the money.

At one point, I stopped next to a certain person and said to the young lady, "You are broke, but you need to help this person. Now, that three hundred dollars in cash is your destiny, and you'd be 'rich' if you ever got there, but right now we've got to go over here."

By the time our hike through the sanctuary ended, that young lady was totally worn out. Nearly every step we took seemed to take her further away from what she was shown to be hers, but in the end she found herself back at the place of her "first revelation."

EXPECT OBSTACLES BUT TRUST HIS PROMISES

How do you deal with the route of destiny? Don't expect a straight route; and if you are smart, you will *expect* to find obstacles blocking your way from time to time. Above all, take comfort in God's promise found in the book of 1 Corinthians:

> *Therefore let him who thinks he stands take heed lest he fall. No temptation has overtaken you but such as is common to man; and God is faithful, who will not allow you to be tempted beyond what you are able, but with the temptation will provide the way of escape also, that you may be able to endure it.* (1 Corinthians 10:12–13 NASB)

Sometimes you won't see the fruit of your labors, the rewards of your sacrifice, or the answers to your prayers in your lifetime; and even the "quicker" situations will tend to be delayed.

Jesus was a baby when Mary heard the prophetic prediction from Simeon about the grief that would pierce her heart, and how the sins of many would be rolled away through her Son.

Thirty-three years later Mary watched her grown Son face false accusations and suffer senseless brutality at the hands of both Jewish and Gentile captors. Then she had to endure the pain of watching her Son be crucified on the cross.

She was party to the transaction of covenant care Jesus orchestrated from the cross with John, but neither she nor John really knew what would happen after Jesus died.

NO ONE DREAMED THEY WOULD
SEE HIM AGAIN

Despite the hints given by Jesus and by the prophets before Him, I don't think that Mary or any of the disciples really anticipated the resurrection. Again, none of them dreamed that they would see Him again on earth—let alone "lose" Him again in the ascension to heaven. Yet, it happened.

We've all heard stories about mothers and grandmothers who prayed faithfully for prodigal sons and daughters, but died before their children and other family members were saved. Personally, I am convinced they get to see the answers to their prayers over the banisters of heaven.

That young lady in my congregation probably wondered if she would ever really get the three hundred dollars I promised her at the beginning of my message. Ultimately, she *did* walk away with that three hundred dollars in cash (and probably collapsed in exhaustion later).

There seems to be a pattern for anyone *elected* by God for a special task or purpose marked by the delivery of divine revelation followed by seasons of silent pondering and private and public suffering.

- Abraham and Sarah pondered the meaning of their covenant promise for twenty-five years, and wrestled with how God would work out that promise. They even attempted to "help" God in their frustration, triggering centuries of interfamily rivalry between the descendants of Ishmael and Isaac. (See Genesis 16:1–4.)

- David must have pondered the meaning of why Samuel anointed him right in front of his father and brothers (the Bible does not say any prophecy was given at that time—see 1 Samuel 16:1–13). Even though he spent time with Samuel later while running from Saul, he still didn't really understand his destiny as Israel's future king. (See 1 Samuel 19:18–20:3.)

- Moses pondered God's words after he discovered the burning bush. (See Exodus 3.) He wrestled with the challenges he faced—challenges that forced him to face his own weaknesses and fears—until he finally rose in full authority in the wilderness, without any real need for his brother's help as spokesman.

- Peter and the other disciples pondered three-and-a-half years' worth of Jesus' teachings and actions. Peter, in particular, surely pondered the things Jesus spoke to him at the most crucial times in his life—the day He called him to come out of the boat and step on the water by faith (Matthew 14:28–33 KJV), the time Jesus praised Peter for seeing His true identity through the Holy Spirit, and moments later said, *"Get thee behind me, Satan"* (Matthew 16:13–33), and His final words spoken after Peter's betrayal and after the Lord's resurrection from the dead, *"Do you love Me?…Feed My sheep"* (John 21:15–19); and later, the revelation by the Spirit that God had included the non-Jewish world in His invitation to eternal life through Christ, the mystery of the cross. (See Acts 10:9–48.)

- Mary of Bethany must have pondered the words of Jesus at Simon the Leper's house, *"When she poured this perfume upon My body, she did it to pre-pare Me for burial;…Wherever this gospel is preached in the whole world, what this woman has done shall also be spoken of in memory of her"* (Matthew 26:12–13 NASB), especially at the cross as she stood with Mary the mother of Jesus and Mary Magdalene. (See John 19:25.)

- Saul the Pharisee, agent of the Sanhedrin, was blinded by a white light and left alone in a room in Damascus, where he pondered for three days what would happen to him after Jesus personally told him in a vision, *"Enter the city, and it shall be told you what you must do"* (Acts 9:6 NASB). God sent a prophet to him and Saul later became the apostle Paul. Evidently, throughout his life Paul pondered the divine revelations he received during visions of the "third heaven"—possibly during his three-year wilderness experience with God in Arabia and Damascus. (See 2 Corinthians 12:1–10 and Galatians 1:11–12, 15–19). The fruit of those revelations is *still* bearing fruit among us to this day!

- The two men walking on the road to Emmaus must have pondered the words of the freshly resurrected Christ for the rest of their lives. The Bible says that after Jesus rebuked them for their unwillingness to believe, *"He explained to them the things concerning Himself in all the Scriptures"* (see Luke 24:13–27 NASB). After Jesus vanished from their sight, they said something that helps us understand what Spirit-inspired "pondering"

really means: ***"Were not our hearts burning within
us*** *while He was speaking to us on the road, while He
was explaining the Scriptures to us?"* (Luke 24:32
NASB, emphasis added).

What is on your "pondering" list? Every Elect Lady has
heard God whisper secrets to her heart if she has stopped long
enough to perceive them. Everyone around you may have said,
"Abort that baby now—it's going to ruin your life. You are too
young—it's *his* fault, anyway. Why should you pay for the rest
of your life for his fifteen minutes of fun?"

God whispers, "This is *your baby*. Protect him with your
life. Cover her with your love—you know what is right. Do it
and trust Me for what you do not know."

The enemy says, "Why should you stick by this man now?
He ran around on you and mistreated you....Why should you
stay with him laid up in bed like that?" The still small voice of
God whispers, "You still love him...*and I love him. I put you two
together so that you can bring him home to Me.*"

Friends and family may say, "Why should you take in those
kids—your sister didn't stay around for them, so why should
you? You have your own family to worry about...and how will
you pay for all of the food and clothes those kids will need?"

A holy whisper blows across your heart, "This is what you
were born for. They will live and become great tomorrow
because you are there for them right now."

Once you hear the whisper of God, you can't turn away
easily. Something in your heart just keeps burning. It keeps
speaking to you night and day. When you are about to give
up, the voice of God echoes in your soul until you get up once
again to face the new day.

Why? It is because you are His Elect Lady.

Chapter 10

From One Elect Lady to Another (First Lady Vanessa Long)

O ne of the most significant events in our ministry together took place the day my husband, Bishop Eddie L. Long, delivered the message "To the Elect Lady" for our annual women's conference.

It was as if God was saying directly to me, "I know you have some disappointments in your life. There were things that I know you wanted. You had painted a picture of what you wanted your husband to be like, and the life you have just doesn't match the picture you carried in your heart for so long. Your life has outgrown your early dreams but remember that *I haven't forgotten you.*"

For many years, our church has sponsored the "Heart to Heart Women's Conference," and I've directed it for the past eight or nine years. Each year when we began planning the conference, I would ask my husband if he would speak for us.

It didn't matter to us whether he opened the conference or delivered the closing address—we knew the women were hungry to hear a word from him just for women.

Looking back, I think he always felt a little uncomfortable about it. He would tell me, "Women wouldn't want to hear anything I have to say." When he finally agreed to speak at the conference, I think the response to the message "To the Elect Lady" took him totally by surprise.

Your life isn't what you dreamed, but God hasn't forgotten you.

The women were so blessed that they *still* talk about that message. I knew it had to be reproduced in book form and felt it would probably be one of his best-selling books because it is so powerful. (And as you probably know, women buy books!)

My husband really touched a nerve in the women present that morning. His strong word from the Lord met them right where they were—myself included. So I was excited when he told me he was going to do a book based on the message, and I even agreed to write this chapter.

Bishop stood to deliver this message at the closing service for the conference on Sunday morning when the conference attendees were joined by our regular congregation members.

SOMETHING SUPERNATURAL HAPPENED

When he read the first words of John's greeting, "To the elect lady..." before that packed house, something supernatural happened that surprised all of us. It was nothing less than a divine "setup" for transformation and visitation.

I've heard my husband minister thousands of times before all kinds of audiences, but I sensed that something was going to be different that morning.

Right from the opening Scripture passage, the women seemed to sense that this really was a word just for them. It seemed as if the Lord was speaking directly to us. The Holy Spirit put His finger on the pulse of the problems and secret pain confronting many of the people seated in the auditorium that morning. Many women today are confronted with disappointment, betrayal, delays, and aborted dreams that threaten to steal any hope they have for a real future.

Almost immediately, the Bishop began talking about the dreams his mother had that were never realized. He shared some of his most private wounds as he talked openly about his mother's sacrifices in life and her current health battles. I know these things are very difficult for him to deal with.

It grieves me as well when I think about my mother-in-law. It hurts to remember the sacrificial life that she lived and to see her suffer from the ravages of progressive dementia now after successfully raising her children and then covering her ailing husband for so many years.

The Bishop's open vulnerability and compassionate understanding of his mother's pain seemed to set the tone for what happened next. The women really opened their hearts to receive his message on a totally different level.

A UNIQUE WORD FOR WOMEN FROM A MAN'S MAN

The women were hungry to hear revelation truth about their lives, and it was unique that it would come from Bishop Eddie L. Long, because those who know my husband will tell you that he is very much a "man's man."

He has a very strong and proven ministry to men on a national and international scale, so when he came forward with this compassionate word for Elect Ladies, it made all of the ladies in the audience feel even more special. God had allowed my husband to be a tool, bringing comfort, healing, and direction that morning.

If you could watch the video of that meeting, you would see the women weep openly and deeply during the message. You could almost feel the release coming from the depths of their souls.

My husband is the Bishop of our church, but he is also my husband, my best friend, and the father of our children. I was blessed to see how the Lord anointed him to be so in tune with the situation so many of us face as women.

CAUGHT OFF GUARD BY VULNERABILITY, POWER, AND COMPASSION

As the Bishop's wife, I used to think that he could be more sensitive to women in general (that is a common view of wives, I suppose). However, it caught me off guard when he became so vulnerable and shared this word with such power and compassion.

There is a lot of pain that goes with ministry, especially when you are married to a pastor, a visionary, or a bishop. But as my husband spoke from the Scriptures, I felt as if the Lord was saying to me and to everyone else who was listening from the heart,

> I think you are special. You are an Elect Lady, and you know I'm going to give grace, mercy, and peace to you. And I know where you are; I haven't forgotten about you. You are special, and I'm using you for My glory.

That's what it said to me personally. I felt God's love, understanding, and compassion comfort my soul through that word. I believe a lot of other women did, too.

I'm sharing what happened to me personally because sometimes it helps people to know how other people cope with the pressures of life.

Elect Lady, you are special, and God is using you for His glory.

A lot of stress automatically comes your way when you marry a man or woman who serves in a very high leadership position. When I first met Eddie Long, he told me that he was the pastor of a Baptist church. For some reason, I thought he had a very small church, and I had no clue that he would become a "big-time preacher." Then I rode by the church building at that time and was in awe of the place. I was thinking, *Oh my goodness! He really is a pastor.*

We met through a mutual friend who worked in the same office building as I did. One day Eddie saw me walking down the street near my office building and asked his friend, "Why don't you introduce me to her?" This mutual friend agreed to set up a blind date with me, but it wasn't fair. Eddie Long already knew who I was.

My Father: "Never Marry a Pastor!"

Once I found out this mystery man was a pastor, I almost backed out of the arrangement because my father (who was also a pastor) strongly encouraged his daughters *not* to marry pastors! He told us it was a difficult life and he didn't want that for us.

Daddy was right—it *is* difficult, but I'm glad I married the man millions of people around the world know as Bishop Eddie L. Long. As it turned out, my father's ministry was dramatically different from my husband's ministry.

My father pastored small churches in south Georgia where the people rarely called their pastor during the week. They seemed to handle their own problems, then simply came together on Sundays for a service. Obviously, my early picture of marriage to a pastor was very different from what I would actually experience.

When I went out with Eddie Long on that blind date, I had already decided I wouldn't go out with this preacher again. But he was so wonderful and made such an impact on me that I agreed to go out with him again. From that point on, the relationship really started to take off.

We kept the relationship somewhat quiet because he really wanted to keep his personal life private, and I certainly understood that. We didn't hide the relationship, but we didn't flaunt it, either.

Although I was a member of another church at that time, I visited his church periodically, being careful not to make it known that we were dating. Theologically, our church backgrounds were a little different in the beginning, too. I was AME [African Methodist Episcopal] before I joined the United Methodist Church in an act of youthful independence. Somehow the differences began to matter less and less.

THEIR CHANCE TO MARRY THE PASTOR WAS OVER!

The New Birth congregation really didn't know about what was happening between us until a Watch Night service when he announced that we were going to get married. (A number of women left the church once we got married because they knew their opportunity to marry the pastor was gone for good.)

I knew that the pastoral ministry could be demanding when we got married, but I wasn't ready for what was coming. At the time about three hundred members attended New Birth Missionary Baptist Church, which met in a much smaller building. We still had some of the traditional trappings of a "normal" family in those days, and we even had dinner together as a family three or four times a week.

Then things started to get busier and busier. My husband began to spend more time with the ministry, and as the church grew, he took outside preaching engagements and traveled more often.

I didn't expect these things to happen at the time we got married. I didn't realize Eddie would be this busy, or that we would become a megachurch.

The success we enjoyed had its good points and its bad ones. I was happy to see the ministry bless so many people, and I was glad to see God use my husband in such a powerful way. On the other hand, I began to notice that our children were missing their daddy. We knew we had to examine our priorities, regroup, reconnect, and put things back on the right road.

It was especially difficult in our blended family because the children were spread across a wide age span. Our youngest child is our daughter, Taylor, who is just entering her teens. Her brother Jared is in his teens. My husband has two sons from his previous marriage: Kodi (who likes to be called Edward now), who is in his twenties, and Eric, his oldest son, who is in his thirties.

We have always had an open-door policy for our children, and they manage to navigate in and out of their daddy's office whenever they need to talk with him.

I DIDN'T EXPECT HIM TO BE GONE SO MUCH

Of course, at that time, Eddie Long wasn't a bishop; he was a local church pastor. Yet even then, I expected to see our young family enjoy a little more home life than we had. Frankly, I didn't expect him to be gone as much as he was. I knew there would be times when he would be called away, but I still hoped that would be the exception and not the rule.

I had to learn how to be married to a leader.

I had to carry the home and children in our blended family. That meant I had to hold things together alone. There were many times over the years that I actually felt like a single parent. Sometimes I tease my husband with the warning, "The next time you ask all the single parents to stand, I'm going to stand, too!"

Sometimes, those who are married to great leaders with great responsibility often battle jealousy over the very things, patterns, or qualities that make them great. When I first met Eddie, he also mentored young men. As I watched him work patiently with these young men, I thought to myself, "Oh, this is great! He's going to be a wonderful father raising our children."

As the years went by and we had our own children, Eddie still had a burning passion for mentoring young leaders. Sometimes we disagreed over how this should balance out. He might say, "Look, our kids are okay. I need to help these kids who are at risk." But I would say, "Okay, but I need you to raise *our* children, too."

I just didn't expect these things when I married Eddie. My husband may be a pastor and bishop now, but he is husband and father first. I thank God for His grace as we worked through these problems (we are like any other married couple, regardless of our particular duties and pressures).

WE CHANGED WHAT WE COULD CHANGE

We had to really talk about the key problem areas—and we had to listen carefully to hear what the other one was saying. So we changed what we could change, and we adapted where we had to.

We set apart one night of the week as family night, and we had to put our family vacations "on the calendar" to make sure they happened.

My husband is anointed and blessed in his ministry because he is absolutely passionate about what he does. There are times when I still have to remind him about certain priorities, because he can get busy traveling. I may have to say, "Okay, wait a minute. Remember that you need to spend a little time at home....You've been gone for three weeks." This crucial balancing act between priorities is just a normal part of life, and we accept that.

Yet, there are still sacrifices and commitments that we cannot avoid or lay aside without laying down God's call and election in our lives. There wasn't any particular turning point, but over the years I began to understand that "this is our life."

I began to understand that I had to let go of some things and trust God. I realized,

> This is our life; this is the way it's going to be. I am a part of this ministry, as large and as overwhelming as it may seem. I have no choice. This is what God has given us, so this is the life we live. And we do it through His grace alone.

If you feel as if you've been left behind, if you have given up, or if you are dealing with the disappointment of delayed dreams to invest in your family or in someone else, I encourage you to keep pressing forward.

GOD WORKS OUT OUR OBEDIENCE AND SIN ISSUES

God will never leave you. Sometimes He may delay fulfilling a desire or need in life because He's trying to work out obedience issues or sin problems in your life.

Above all, trust in God and never give up. Do what Paul did—"Forget what lies behind and reach forward to what lies ahead. *'Press on toward the goal for the prize of the upward call of God in Christ Jesus.'*" (See Philippians 3:14 NASB.)

You may never realize all of your childhood dreams or even the dreams of your maturity, but this is not fatal. If you place your life in God's hands and your dreams aren't realized, then in some way you will find that you have exchanged *your* dream for God's dream.

It doesn't mean that God doesn't love you. Sometimes He tries to do something different through you to bless someone else (just as He did through Jesus). Someone else may be virtually paralyzed with disappointment—perhaps they will learn how they can make it through *by watching you.*

> Look over there...do you see Vanessa? She didn't realize her personal dreams but she's still living that abundant life. Do you see Maria over there? She's had her share of disappointments and surprises, but she is trying to press forward. She refuses to simply sit there dying and depressed, content with the lie that her life is over.

HAVE YOU SEEN THE "HUXTABLE FAMILY"?

When the day is over and every opinion has been given, it's not about me or you. It is all about Him and drawing others to His love.

Place your life in God's hand, and He will make His dream your dream.

Again, before I met Bishop Long, I dreamed of having a marriage with a traditional family life (which in part meant we would spend *a lot of time together* as a family). My husband sometimes jokes that I was looking for the "Huxtable family" (the upscale, urban African-American television family in the situation comedy created and produced by Dr. Bill Cosby).

We do raise the kids together, but not as "together" as I'd dreamed. Now I realize that God is giving me grace because my life today is part of my *election* in Christ. Looking back at our early years of marriage, I can really see His grace at work.

When God elects you to raise children in a blended family situation—whether it occurs because of the death of a spouse or through divorce—there are special difficulties that must be overcome.

For one thing, I came from a family in which all of the children were girls. God arranged for me to step into a "ready-made family" composed entirely of males. As I struggled to make the adjustment, my husband tried to encourage me, saying, "Well, boys are different, you know. You just have to handle them differently from girls."

Of course, I didn't have a clue what I had inherited by marriage. In the beginning, I was trying to raise kids without ever having had any children of my own. Early in our marriage, my husband's youngest son, Kodi, still lived with his mother most of the time. Yet, his mother was a flight attendant who had to deal with a work schedule that might change at a moment's notice—and the times involved were almost always inconvenient.

The irritation factor really kicked in when my husband received those middle-of-the-night phone calls: "Could you come and get Kodi? I have to go to work."

I just couldn't understand how Eddie could stay so calm and make such sacrifices over and over again. It annoyed me in the beginning and I'd ask, "Why do you have to go get Kodi in the middle of the night?"

Everything seemed to change when I gave birth to Jared. Finally I began to truly understand what it meant to say, "This is my child. I have to be there for him." From that point on, things began to work out.

Then I faced the challenge of adjusting to the changing personality of "Eric the teenager." I can honestly say that Eric was never disrespectful—it was just that I didn't know anything about teenagers!

When God elects you to do the difficult and achieve the impossible, the process of walking it out will drive you to your knees in prayer. When you end up with more challenge than you have courage, your need to lean on God will deepen and enrich your relationship with Him. It is a natural byproduct of diligent search and struggle; it is the fruit of an honest heart-cry to God.

The Lord strengthened the weak areas in my life, and my husband and I realize that God put us together so we would strengthen and challenge one another in our calling. As my husband became busier and busier, I had to grow spiritually just to carry the increased load of operating our household as the primary parent.

God brought us together to challenge one another.

My husband really felt there were things in my heart as a woman that had to come out. He knew there was leadership in me, and he encouraged me to share some of the powerful things God placed within me.

It Was a Monumental Moment

The morning Eddie delivered this message on "The Elect Lady" marked the beginning of a birthing process that helped me become the leader I am right now. It was a monumental moment in my life.

Once I accepted who I am and embraced the basic truths in this message, I felt a release from deep within my soul. God was telling me it was all right to let my guard down and openly admit to the members of our church that I face challenges just like they do. I was tired of hiding behind a religious façade of perfection while pretending that everything was okay. God wanted people to see that I was a normal person who has to lean on God every day just like they do.

Finally, the day came when my husband laid his hands on me publicly as Bishop and pastor, and he spoke into my life by the power of the Holy Spirit. This became a powerful affirmation to me of who I am.

I knew that there was something more to me, but I needed the extra affirmation. I am not too proud to say I wanted my husband to recognize the gift of God in me. It blessed me to hear my husband and the leader of our church say, "This is what God has done in your life, and I have faith in you to fulfill His will. I believe in you." (This may not make much sense to some people, and I know it may enrage the feminists and certain insecure females, but this is how God did it in my life!)

YOU DID IT FOR OTHERS—WHAT ABOUT ME?

I remember telling my husband one month earlier, "I've seen you lay hands on so many different people. You speak into their lives and publicly affirm who they are in Christ, but you haven't done that with me."

He told me later that he quickly realized God had done a real work in me, and decided to publicly seal and endorse what the Lord had done by laying hands on me and ordaining me as a minister in the church.

Mary is the woman in the Bible whose story most inspires and encourages me as an Elect Lady. Her answer to the Lord has become my answer: "Let it be unto me, Lord, according to Your will." (See Luke 1:38.)

My heart goes out to the millions of women who struggle to survive and preserve the futures of fractured families, dependent children, adopted or foster children, elderly parents, disabled spouses, and grandchildren.

Women are so relational that they can be hurt deeply through broken relationships. They suffer extreme pain and disappointment when they feel betrayed by men or by other women who are close to them.

Loneliness haunts every waking hour for many single women trying to raise children. Divorce can deprive them of loved ones, income, security, and hope for the future. Many women stay in their marriages but feel trapped and without any hope for change and breakthrough. Many of them have to give up their dreams of owning their own homes, or to land better jobs.

Everyone is faced with the same decision in times of disappointment or crisis: Will I continue to dwell on what I don't have, or will I decide to go on and live?

DON'T FORFEIT YOUR FUTURE!

Everything moves forward or backward from that one decision. What is really significant in your life? What do you want to accomplish? If you decide to focus on what you do *not* have, you automatically forfeit your future. Your destination is locked in—you are going to get bitter, not better.

If you choose to go and live, then you have positioned yourself to reclaim your future. I *know* that God wants to bless us and provide the things we need. However, the way we wait on God often determines how *long* we wait. It all comes down to our attitude and our faith. Choose life, and *believe* the truth that God can bless you.

He cannot and will not bless you as long as you dwell on what you don't have. You will "dine" on past disappointments and offenses every day and every night until you choose something else on the menu of life. Once you put your trust in Him, you activate the key of faith to release all of the resources of heaven.

In the process, your life becomes a beacon of hope for everyone around you. Do you have friends who struggle with things that just don't seem "fair" in life? Understand that God uses *your life* to encourage them and let them know that He still loves them.

ENDNOTES

Special note: God elects some ladies to bear very special children under extremely difficult circumstances. (This might include women such as Mary, Sarah, Rachel, Ruth, and Hannah.)

His divine election may also include single mothers who face the difficult task of raising children alone, and grandmothers who spend their golden years raising their grandchildren. Mothers (and fathers) who faithfully raise special needs children or care for aged parents are also elect and special in the eyes of God.

There is yet another category of Elect Ladies who are called to marry and raise families with men called to sacrificial ministries in the kingdom of God (this seems to be where I fit in). These ministries come in all sizes, types, and places (they are not limited to megachurches or international ministry organizations). Some of these women share the ministry with their husbands, and others focus primarily on support and leadership in the home. (Again, Mary, Elizabeth, Sarah, Rachel, and Hannah would fit into this category.)

Still another group of Elect Ladies are themselves called to sacrificial leadership functions in the kingdom, and find support in their spouses or some other source. (This would include Mary, Esther, and Deborah, the Old Testament *"mother in Israel"* and judge who, with Barak, led her nation to victory over its enemies. See Judges 4–5.)

Chapter 11

"Ain't God Good?" The Power of the Encouraging Word

During the time when I was preparing to go into the ministry in Richmond, Virginia, I went through a crisis that completely robbed me of every desire to preach. Like most folks who find themselves in a crisis, I really wanted to go to church. The pastor at the church I was attending, Rev. O. D. Brown, was a good man of God, and he befriended me.

I soon learned that Rev. Brown had another spiritual "asset" that would have even greater impact on my life. This secret weapon was an elderly lady named Miss Beatrice Jones, who served as the pastor's housekeeper—and his prayer covering.

When Rev. Brown passed away, Miss Jones was left without a job or a home of her own. (She lived in a retirement home located next to the church where Rev. O. D. Brown used to serve as pastor.) In His great favor, God linked her heart with mine, and Miss Jones began to pray for me—a better way to say it is that she "adopted me" in prayer. In fact, she became like a "Big Mama" to me in the spirit (at the time of this writing, she was ninety-seven years old).

We talked often, especially in crucial times. Sometimes I would call her just before I preached, or if I was feeling down for some reason (and it happens).

Miss Jones didn't call me Bishop—in fact, she never called me Bishop, that I recall. She was from the old school, and she always referred to me as "Brother."

Nearly every time I called, Miss Jones started off the conversation the same way. Perhaps she did it because she sensed where I was through my responses.

"How you doing, Reverend?"

"I'm fine, Miss Jones."

"Remember when I met you?"

"Yes, ma'am."

"Nobody thought you'd go this far, did they?"

"No ma'am."

"Ain't God good? You never imagined you'd be pastoring a church of 25,000, did you?"

"No, ma'am."

"Did you ever think you might be one of those 'bishops'?"

"No, ma'am."

"You never thought you'd be on television, or flyin' over the ocean to minister to Africans and Australians, did you?"

"No, ma'am."

"Ain't God good?"

ONE SUBJECT FOR EVERY OCCASION: "AIN'T GOD GOOD?"

Miss Jones always reminded me of the things she has seen happen in my life over the years. And no matter what came up in our conversation, and no matter what problem I brought up in our talk, I could count on Miss Jones. She had one subject for every occasion. No matter where we began, our conversation always ended with a focus on one truth above all others: "Ain't God good?"

By the time Miss Jones stepped into her anointing as an encourager and talked to me about God's goodness for fifteen or twenty minutes straight, I usually couldn't even remember what I was calling her about! Every problem simply disappeared under the flood of praise she released toward God.

Problems disappeared under a flood of praise.

Miss Jones carried an anointing to change the whole atmosphere overhead when she talked to me. She did it all the time, and she always let me know just how proud she was of me (and I appreciate it!).

"I'm just so proud of you, Brother. And don't you know that every time I get on my knees, Reverend, I pray for you. And the Lord has got you in His hand! Now I'm *always* praying for you."

160

ENCOURAGEMENT MAKES THE DIFFERENCE BETWEEN FAILURE AND SUCCESS

Over and over again, I've thanked the Lord for linking my heart with a ninety-seven-year-old encourager who was anointed by the Holy Spirit! She literally made the difference between success and failure at key times in my life and ministry. No one is meant to go through life as an island, alone and totally independent from the support and input of others. (Some of us are just too proud or foolish to acknowledge it!)

Miss Jones dedicated her whole life to the ministry of intercession and encouragement. She never owned her own home or held a lot of possessions. She was nothing less than a gift from God to this preacher from Atlanta.

Men, women, and even the only begotten Son of God have benefited from the power of encouragement and the encouraging word.

Never underestimate the power of an encouraging word! True encouragers are people who keep their spirits clean. They are above reproach and their motives are pure without a doubt.

It is important to understand that the primary difference between flattery and encouragement is purity of heart.

It seems that very few Christians keep their "inward man" totally clean, but it is purity of spirit and the absence of private agendas that qualifies and equips these special encouragers to relate properly to individuals and leaders. God gives them the grace to remain untouched by fame, personal ambition, or the size of a person's ministry. Where would we be without people like that?

Among other things, the Bible is God's record of the supernatural encouragement He has given to His servants in the heavens and on the earth in times of spiritual battle, distress, and crisis.

The Hebrew word most often translated as "encouragement" is *chazaq*. It can mean:

> To fasten upon; hence to seize, be strong (figuratively, to be courageous, to strengthen, cure, help, repair, fortify), obstinate [one of my favorites]; to bind, restrain, conquer—to aid, catch, cleave, confirm, be constant, continue, be of good courage, to encourage, to be established, fasten, force, make hard, help, lean, maintain, play the man, mend, become mighty, be stout, to make strong, to be sure, to take hold, be urgent, to behave yourself valiantly, to withstand.[1]

Now, any of these definition components will "preach" because there is so much *power* released through the encouraging word.

THIS WAS GOD'S FINAL TOPIC FOR LIFE

When Moses came to the end of the forty-year wilderness journey and prepared to hand the reins of rule to Joshua, God's final topic was encouragement:

> *Go up to the top of Pisgah and lift up your eyes to the west and north and south and east, and see it with your eyes, for you shall not cross over this Jordan. But charge Joshua and **encourage him and strengthen him**; for he shall go across at the head of this people, and he shall give them as*

an inheritance the land which you will see.
(Deuteronomy 3:27–28 NASB, emphasis added)

God wanted Moses to strengthen and fortify his replacement so Joshua would become obstinate about binding and conquering God's enemies. The message of encouragement was to be the final earthly message delivered by one of God's greatest prophets and leaders!

Moses was to deliver his word of encouragement to help Joshua be constant, courageous, hardened (for battle), mighty, stout, and strong so he could take hold and seize God's Promised Land while he himself valiantly stood, prevailed, and withstood every challenge!

Daniel the prophet had to stand alone as an intercessor on behalf of his people most of his life while he served foreign kings as a captive of Babylon and Persia.

The Hebrew word, *chazaq*, appears many times in the book of Daniel describing interchanges between angel and archangel and archangel and man—and they all involve *encouragement* or *strengthening* (you get *both* meanings in the original Hebrew word).

YOU HAVE STRENGTHENED ME!

In Daniel 10, the prophet received an angelic visitation (it was probably Jesus Himself as the "Angel of the Lord"), and the shock of God's glory caused Daniel to faint. In fact, Daniel continued to tremble uncontrollably once he was revived. Only after the angelic being spoke an *encouraging word* to Daniel was he was finally able to speak:

And he said, "O man of high esteem, do not be afraid. Peace be with you; take courage [chazaq] and be courageous

[chazaq]!" Now **as soon as he spoke to me, I received strength** *[chazaq] and said, "May my lord speak,* **for you have strengthened** *[chazaq]* **me.***"
(Daniel 10:19 NASB, emphasis added)

When the angel described his cosmic battle with the demon prince over Persia, he said, *"Yet there is no one who* **stands firmly** *[chazaq] with me against these forces except Michael your prince* [the archangel of God]" (Daniel 10:21 NASB, emphasis added).

The New Testament gospels and epistles also speak constantly about the power and necessity of encouragement and the encouraging word.

God chose Barnabas to take Saul of Tarsus under his wing, and his name literally means "Son of Encouragement," according to the writer of Acts! (See Acts 4:36.)

The Word of God is your source of strength.

One early apostolic letter to new Christians at Antioch brought rejoicing because of the encouragement or *"consolation"* (KJV) it brought to the people. (See Acts 15:22–31.)

In his letter to the Romans, Paul spoke of the *"encouragement* ["comfort" (NKJV)] *of the Scriptures"* (Romans 15:4 NASB). This was one of the most prominent apostolic letters to early believers and followers of Christ.

GOD'S WORD: "ENCOURAGEMENT 101"

All of the Scriptures we have received are God's Word passed directly to us. The Word of God should be one of your greatest sources of encouragement and strength! The Bible is your personal strength class, "Encouragement 101."

In Romans 15:5 (NASB), Paul also said God Himself *"gives perseverance and encouragement."*

I can tell you from years of personal experience that this verse is absolutely true! Many times, when I was feeling overwhelmed, outgunned, and under-equipped, I remember feeling God's presence enfold me like a blanket of strength and encouragement.

At other times He sent people into my life with a brotherly hug, an encouraging word, or a prophetic exhortation at just the right time to "keep on keeping on, no matter the cost."

This is what Paul was talking about when he wrote,

> *If therefore there is any encouragement in Christ, if there is any consolation of love, if there is any fellowship of the Spirit, if any affection and compassion, make my joy complete by being of the same mind, maintaining the same love, united in spirit, intent on one purpose. Do nothing from selfishness or empty conceit, but with humility of mind let each of you regard one another as more important than himself; do not merely look out for your own personal interests, but also for the interests of others.* (Philippians 2:1–4 NASB)

ENCOURAGERS ARE GIFTED TO DO WHAT FEW DARE TO DO

God's Elect Ladies have a high calling to serve as lifelong encouragers to *others* (to children, grandchildren, stepchildren, wounded or dysfunctional spouses, or elderly parents). They seem to be gifted from heaven with the ability to do what very few others would dare to do and what almost no one wants to do.

The Lord gives all of us the grace to do His will in life, but Elect Ladies need a special measure of mercy and grace just

165

to survive. Some of His greatest gifts to Elect Ladies come in the form of other anointed encouragers and comforters sent alongside them in times of need.

The Elect Lady in my life, Vanessa, is a great encouragement and help to me. I couldn't fulfill my calling without her, but *my* encourager needs as much or more encouragement than I do. As her husband, friend, and life partner, it is my responsibility to be her chief encourager.

We all have Elect Ladies in our lives, but are we doing everything God calls us to do for them?

Do you obey that gentle prompting to call "Widow Jones" to make sure there is enough food in the house for her and her grandchildren? What happens when God speaks to you at some "inconvenient time" about dropping your schedule and grabbing a friend to visit the single mother who lives nearby? (If you think about it, almost *any* time is inconvenient, so why worry about the inconvenience at all?)

HAS GOD SPOKEN TO YOU ABOUT HIS ELECT LADIES?

How many times have the men in our churches failed to recognize that it was *God* who was speaking to them about His Elect Ladies? It was the Lord telling you, "Son, forget those Saturday plans. Go see the lady with three sons who have no father. Rearrange your schedule to take them to the ball game or fishing this weekend. They need a man's voice in their life."

Someday we may learn that heartbroken mothers have been pouring out their souls in prayer, asking God to send Christ-loving men to teach their sons how to be men. We'll hear about the grandmothers who bombarded heaven with prayers for someone to fix the leaky roof on the house and replace the broken flooring so the grandchildren they are raising will have a decent place to grow up.

The best answer, in *every situation,* is for us to obey God's voice. You and I may become God's blessing in a time of need. If we have the opportunity to bring hope and joy into the lives of His Elect Ladies, there is a special blessing waiting in heaven for us.

It is best to obey God's voice in every situation.

Many of these Elect Ladies qualify literally, or spiritually, as widows. And those they care for often qualify as "orphans" in the sight of God. Do you remember what God says about these two groups of people?

> *This is pure and undefiled religion in the sight of our God and Father,* **to visit orphans and widows in their distress***, and to keep oneself unstained by the world.*
> (James 1:27 NASB, emphasis added)

THE ENCOURAGER'S ANTHEM

The apostle Paul faced impossible obstacles and dangerous persecution for most of his ministry, yet he is the one who penned what I have to believe is "The Encourager's Anthem" for my prayer warrior friend and countless others like her:

> *Rejoice in the Lord always; again I will say, rejoice! Let your forbearing spirit be known to all men. The Lord is near. Be anxious for nothing, but in everything by prayer and supplication with thanksgiving let your requests be made known to God. And the peace of God, which surpasses all comprehension, shall guard your hearts and your minds in*

Christ Jesus. Finally, brethren, whatever is true, whatever is honorable, whatever is right, whatever is pure, whatever is lovely, whatever is of good repute, if there is any excellence and if anything worthy of praise, let your mind dwell on these things. (Philippians 4:4–8 NASB)

Every time Miss Jones invaded my weary night of the soul with her encouraging light, my world began to change! The day may have begun in gloom and doom, but by the time Miss Jones finished her task of lifting up praise to God and describing His glory, my day was on its way to total victory.

God is good.

All the time.

"Ain't God good?"

"Oh, I don't know...."

"Don't know? Why this is the God who hung the moon and the stars in the velvety expanse of space. It was God—*your God*—who crafted and formed you while you were still in your mama's womb!

"It was God who first whispered your name into the universe, and it was that same God who gave you your *first* breath...and He is the God who will be there with His scarred hand extended to lead you home when you take your *last* breath!

"Ain't God good? Of *course* He is! Because God so loved you that He gave His only begotten Son, that whosoever—and that means *you*soever—believes on Him shall not die, but have everlasting life.

"Oh, you know alright. God *is* good—all the time."

Never underestimate the power of encouraging words. Receive them when they come, and be ready to give them to others at the slightest urging of the Holy Spirit.

The encouraging word is so important that it was mentioned by the prophet Isaiah as essential equipment for the Savior of the world, Jesus Christ:

> *The Sovereign Lord has given me his words of wisdom,* ***so that I know what to say to*** *[how to encourage]* ***all these weary ones***. *Morning by morning he wakens me and opens my understanding to his will. The Sovereign Lord has spoken to me, and I have listened. I do not rebel or turn away.* (Isaiah 50:4–5 NLT, emphasis added)

ENDNOTES

1. James Strong, *Strong's Exhaustive Concordance of the Bible* (Peabody, MA: Hendrickson Publishers, n.d.). Adapted from the complete word definition provided for "encouragement" (Hebrew #2388, *chazaq*).

Chapter 12

Preparing the Next Generation of Elect Ones

S ometimes you have to give up things you value to give birth to or to nurture things of even greater value.

Ask any mother—especially a single mother who must face the future alone. Ask any grandmother, aunt, or cousin who has sacrificed her personal freedoms and privileges to raise grandchildren, nephews, nieces, or second cousins. Ask any adult child who has sacrificed things to care for an ill or incapacitated elderly parent.

Where children and their destinies are concerned, sacrifice just seems to be a permanent part of the equation. Selfish people don't do a good job of raising children, and most of them bail out quickly or find ways to "dump" the responsibilities of parenting on others. The same thing could be said about aged parents and their destinies. (This is where God's Elect Ladies come in most often.)

When someone like Mary agrees to pay the price, her personal sacrifice for the sake of others touches countless lives in the generations to come.

Even if this were the only reason, we must say that no sacrifice is too great. But there are many more reasons, and the first and greatest reason is that it is *right*.

How do we help prepare the next generation of God's elect ones? Exactly how do you train young people to live sacrificially? What makes a young woman like Mary so willing to lay down her hopes and dreams for the sake of others? (Most of our society rebels at the very thought of this.)

To me it is simple—this "equation" begins and ends with God. The Bible says, *"For **it is God** who is at work in you, both **to will** and **to work** for His good pleasure"* (Philippians 2:13 NASB, emphasis added).

Love was Jesus' motivation in all things.

Beyond that, we can follow in the footsteps of Jesus and learn from the many ways He prepared twelve men and a significant number of women for a takeover of the world system. It takes time to point out to others the different paradigms or ways of thinking Jesus demonstrated in His life, death, and resurrection.

The Lord Jesus did everything from two motivations. First, He was obedient to His Father in all things. Second, He loved us. Love was His supreme motivation in all things—even when He brought correction or rebuke.

171

If you hope to develop leaders, risk-takers, and sacrificial Elect Ladies, then refuse to accept or adopt any shortcuts or mixed motives.

REAL-TIME, HANDS-ON, UP CLOSE AND PERSONAL DEMONSTRATION

Theory and classroom instruction aren't enough where genuine work and personal sacrifice are required. We must give the next generation nothing less than a real-time, hands-on, up close and personal demonstration of what it means to die to self for the good of others.

Jesus did it. He spent *time* with the disciples in the field, in the synagogues, in the temple, and among the surging crowds of needy people. He used everyday events, real ministry assignments, and difficult obstacles and situations to teach and train the Twelve.

His goal? He was determined to teach them how to do what He did. He equipped His disciples to follow in His footsteps and succeed in the real world—long after He had returned to the Father.

That brings up a disturbing question for most of us: "Am I doing something worthy to pass on to others?"

Understand this: the need is there. Mentorship may have become "politically incorrect" in the world, but it is still God's ordained way for training upcoming generations. Even the business world seems to be catching on—*finally.*

SEPARATING THE ELECTED FROM THE ENTITLED

While watching a recent TV news program on the so-called "Entitlement Generation," I heard a number of experts, authors, social researchers, and employers describe some of the characteristics of the younger generation entering America's workforce and college ranks.

Many of America's young people are highly skilled consumers who know what they want, how to find good deals, and where to buy staggering amounts of goods and services. They move fast and do much of their purchasing with credit cards over the Internet.

They also seem to be unusually motivated to succeed—unlike the so-called "X-generation slackers" before them. They seem to compete more aggressively than earlier generations, at least partially because they like *things*.

Members of this "entitlement generation" automatically assume they will succeed because they've enjoyed all of the trappings of success so early in their lives. (A pediatric professor interviewed on the program placed the blame on "coddling parents" and unpractical course offerings in colleges and universities.)

Follow the perfect example of Jesus, who always told the truth.

They expect good jobs to be waiting for them, and they expect good wages, excellent benefits, and all of the privileges of power *from the moment they are hired*. One consultant calls the job applicants "kidployees" to help employers understand what they are facing.[1]

My impression at the end of the program was that most of the people interviewed felt the members of the "entitlement generation" were in for some very unpleasant and unexpected surprises. They will have to make some very painful adjustments in their lifestyles in the future.

How do we separate out and help prepare the next generation of God's elect ones if the concept of sacrifice and diligence over the long haul is missing from their character? We follow the perfect example of Jesus, who always told the truth.

GREAT NEWS—YOU *WILL* BE PERSECUTED

Jesus did *not* tell the disciples that once they agreed to follow Him, everything in life would go their way. Nor did the apostle Paul. He described the ways he suffered for preaching the gospel, and added, *"Indeed, all who desire to live godly in Christ Jesus **will be persecuted**"* (2 Timothy 3:12 NASB, emphasis added).

If that isn't enough to make us think about our commitment, we should consider the implications of what Jesus said:

> *Remember the word that I said to you, "A slave is not greater than his master." If they persecuted Me, **they will also persecute you**.* (John 15:20 NASB, emphasis added)

The Lord did *not* say:

"If you really want to follow Me, just raise your hand while everyone's head is bowed—don't worry, nobody will see you.

"Now everything will be fine—you've got your lifetime pass to 'JesusWorld'—just live like you want to live because My grace will cover you like grease in a skillet. I want you to be free to be you—even if it makes you less like Me.

"Express your every desire and explore every lust. I've already covered any sin you might commit, so just live like the devil and lean on the grease—I mean, grace.

"Never say no to yourself; that might harm your emerging self-esteem.

"And since you belong to My love club, nobody will ever do anything bad to you, cuss you out, cheat you, or threaten to kill you. After all, you are a child of God—who could hate you?"

He *did* say something that most Christians overlook, ignore, or avoid most of their lives:

> If anyone wishes to come after Me, **let him deny himself,** *and* **take up his cross daily***, and follow Me. For whoever wishes to save his life* **shall lose it***, but* **whoever loses his life for My sake***, he is the one who will* **save it***.*
>
> (Luke 9:23–24 NASB, emphasis added)

Jesus trained His disciples to be filled with eternal hope but to live by faith. He was also careful to warn them in simple and blunt terms that hard times would come. We need to impart these truths to the next generation so they will understand that Christianity isn't supposed to be easy, but God sees us through the hard times.

How Do You Handle Disappointments?

If you really want to prepare your children, grandchildren, and other young people around you to succeed in Christ, then make sure you also teach them how to handle the disappointments that may come in life.

How do you do that? You teach them how to:

1. hear God's voice for themselves.

2. fall in love with Him.

3. honor His Word above every human opinion or conclusion.

Even highly successful people who are spared such life-stressing challenges as divorce, disease, or tragedy *will* face frustrations, opposition, and broken dreams. No one can avoid them completely.

What are you teaching or passing on to the people around you through your words and deeds? Are you truthfully preparing them for life's sometimes painful realities? Is your life a living book of instruction and training demonstrating the power of God to keep and preserve in times of crisis, or a warning sign that says, "Unsafe at any speed"?

At the very least, the people God places in your life should be learning these key principles:

- Life isn't a movie. Sometimes you just won't be rescued by the proverbial knight in shining armor.

- God is good, and He *will* honor every promise He has made to you; but it is inevitable that you will be hurt by other people in the course of life.

- Even the best human beings among us fail to measure up to His standards. Do you know what you will you do when bad things happen?

Some things to work on include considering where you will turn if your "hoped-for hero or heroine" fails to show up when you most expected an appearance. Will your faith crumble or will it grow stronger in a crisis?

CRISIS AND FAILURE SHOULD NEVER PERMANENTLY DISQUALIFY THE REPENTANT

A painful crisis or a failure in life may temporarily pull you out of active service to God in a public role, but if you have a heart like David—a heart of repentance that is focused on pleasing God more than man—then crises or failures should never permanently disqualify you from service to the King.

For instance, I know many good Christians who have struggled through the painful process of divorce—I am one of them! Do I say that everyone should go through a divorce so they can experience a wonderful remarriage? Absolutely not! If you marry, plan for your marriage to last for life—but anchor your life in Jesus Christ and God's Word.

(If your marriage should run into trouble, a solid foundation in Christ and the Word will become your most important source for the strength and wisdom needed to save that marriage. If it fails despite every effort, your foundation in Christ and in God's kingdom will help you regain your feet and start over by faith.)

God is at work in each of us to help us do the impossible.

What does this have to do with God's Elect Ladies? Many, if not most, Elect Ladies have been pulled out of public ministry by family circumstances, unplanned pregnancies as unwed mothers, economic failures, or even by previous criminal activity. My point is simple: There is still power in the cross and in the blood of Jesus Christ to forgive sin and remove its memory from God's record!

TRADE YOUR VIEWPOINT FOR GOD'S VIEWPOINT

What about sacrifice and diligence in the long haul? Anyone who really wants to follow Jesus and please God must understand that he may have to give up certain things for a bigger picture from God's viewpoint. The good news is that God is at work in each of us to help us do the impossible.

Once again, it is Jesus' words that move us away from society's materialistic norm, which seems to shout from every corner, "Everything is for *me*, and *right now!*"

Jesus sees things differently. He put it this way:

Do not be anxious then, saying, "What shall we eat?" or "What shall we drink?" or "With what shall we clothe ourselves?" [What about me, me, me? I want new clothes, right now.] *For all these things the Gentiles eagerly seek; for your heavenly Father knows that you need all these things. But* **seek first His kingdom** [rather than just His blessings] *and His righteousness* [rather than just His benefits and promises]*; and all these things shall be added to you.*   (Matthew 6:31–33 NASB, emphasis added)

HIS PATTERN HAS BECOME OUR PATTERN— FROM DEATH TO LIFE

The Lord painted another word picture describing the path of death and rebirth He would take. We all are destined to imitate this pattern in our own lives by faith as we die to self, take up our cross, and follow Him. (See Luke 9:23.) I'm quoting from the New Living Translation because its version of this passage makes Jesus' words come alive to us:

The truth is, a kernel of wheat must be planted in the soil. Unless it dies it will be alone—a single seed. But its death will produce many new kernels—a plentiful harvest of new lives. Those who love life in this world will lose it. Those who despise their life in this world will keep it for eternal life.   (John 12:24–25 NLT)

From my earliest days as an adult follower of Jesus Christ, I've been compelled by God's love to invest my life in the lives of hundreds of young men and women. It came naturally, but it still required sacrifice, commitment, and all of my resources (plus God's abundant supply) to equip, train, and empower them to influence the lives of others for the kingdom.

The Bible is filled with powerful examples of people—men and women—who invested time, energy, and resources to *prepare others* who were destined to be Elect Ladies or Elect Men of God.

As I mentioned earlier, Naomi was widowed and alone in a foreign land when her calling to be God's *Elect Lady* caught up with her. As a woman approaching old age, she had lost what appeared to be a secure future after her husband died prematurely, only to be followed in death by her two adult sons.

ROBBED BY DEATH, INTIMIDATED BY LIFE

Death had robbed her of any hope of income; her ability to sustain life in a foreign land was gone for good. She was left with two grieving daughters-in-law who were nearly as destitute as she was. To make matters worse, both women were Moabites who had been trained from childhood to be loyal to other gods. Naomi found herself in the same place that haunts many of God's Elect Ladies—they are robbed by death (or by sin or painful circumstances) and intimidated by life (living alone with little hope for a future).

Since Naomi had no inheritance to offer her daughters-in-law, no grandchildren to raise and preserve the memory of her husband and sons, and no way of feeding or housing the two younger women, she encouraged them to go home to their families and start over.

Somehow, God imparted something supernatural to Ruth through the influence of Naomi and her late husband and sons.

She willingly laid aside all of her dreams and her ancestral gods (something that just wasn't done in her culture) to embrace the invisible God worshiped by her late husband's family.

NAOMI AND RUTH BOTH ACCEPTED THEIR ELECTION

Love compelled Ruth to step into *her own election* in God by willingly leaving her own family and Moabite heritage behind to follow her mother-in-law, Naomi, to Bethlehem. It was here that she would meet and marry Boaz, and together they brought a son named Jesse into the world.

Naomi also acted as an Elect Lady when she agreed to take in and mentor her widowed daughter-in-law, Ruth. Her act of faith opened the door for Ruth, as an Elect Lady, to match with Boaz and deliver a boy named Jesse.

> *Love compelled Ruth to step into her own election.*

When Jesse grew up and married, he and his wife gave Ruth eight grandsons—including his youngest son, *David*.

It was through King David that God transformed the history of Israel and Judah, and ushered in the coming of His Son, Jesus the Messiah. So it was through the obedience of two obscure Elect Ladies that God brought about the fulfillment of prophecy spanning thousands of years!

God positioned Naomi as an Elect Lady, who then covered and delivered Ruth. It was through Ruth—a widowed foreigner who started out far from God—that the Lord transformed human history. This Elect Lady was placed at exactly the right place and time to deliver a son and an anointed grandson into the world in perfect unison with God's plan for mankind.

THE UNCLE AND THE ELECT LADY

Let's look at another example of mentorship. Mordecai the Jew served in the royal court of the powerful Persian king, Xerxes, but he transformed history by adopting, raising, and directing an *Elect Lady* named Esther into her destiny.

This man actually faced many of the same challenges single mothers, single fathers, and guardians face today! He adopted Esther, his younger cousin, after her parents died of unexplained causes. For many years, he raised Esther alone. Just as she reached marriageable age, the king of Persia had a sudden vacancy at the palace—he deposed (or disposed of) his previous queen and began a kingdom-wide search for a replacement. He ordered that all the beautiful young virgins in the Persian Empire be brought to the royal palace as candidates for queen.

Mordecai knew that Esther had no choice, and he was powerless to intervene. King Xerxes commanded what had become the most powerful empire on earth at the time, and he was accustomed to having his royal commands obeyed instantly.

As Esther prepared to go to the king's palace in Susa, Mordecai advised her not to tell anyone she was Jewish or that she was related to him. After a year of preparation and some extra time awaiting her turn to be with the king, Esther was chosen over all of the other young women to become queen of Persia.

Things went well for some time, but the king still didn't realize that Esther was Jewish or related to Mordecai. The cousins carefully preserved the secret, even though Queen Esther passed along a tip from Mordecai that saved King Xerxes from an assassination plot hatched by his own bodyguards.

Some time went by, and then a foreigner named Haman was suddenly promoted to the number two position by King Xerxes. When Mordecai refused to bow to him (not only was Haman descended from the mortal enemies of the Jews, but to do so would be to break the first commandment), Haman decided to get revenge. He decided the best way to strike at Mordecai was to engineer the mass destruction of *all* the Jews in Persia, and in the middle of a drinking party he convinced King Xerxes to sign a decree authorizing his scheme.

> *Who knows? Maybe you were born for such a time as this.*

When Mordecai discovered the plot, he tore his clothes, refused to eat any food, and covered himself in ashes in a public place. When Queen Esther heard that Mordecai was sitting in a public square covered in ashes, she sent a messenger to find out what had happened as she could not leave the royal quarters.

THIS ELECT LADY RISKED HER LIFE TO SAVE HER PEOPLE

The messenger relayed Mordecai's story to the queen, along with the news that she would have to risk her life and violate royal law to save her people. When Queen Esther balked, Mordecai sent her a message that still reverberates across the ages to every Elect Lady of God:

> *Think not with thyself that thou shalt escape in the king's house, more than all the Jews. For if thou altogether hold-est thy peace at this time, then shall there enlargement and deliverance arise to the Jews from another place; but thou and thy father's house shall be destroyed:* **and who knoweth**

> ***whether thou art come to the kingdom for such a time***
> ***as this?*** (Esther 4:13–14 KJV, emphasis added)

Esther agreed to go before King Xerxes despite the standing sentence of death for anyone who entered the Persian king's court without invitation. She tapped God's wisdom to know how to break the news of Haman's plot; and in the end, God gave His Elect Lady supernatural favor.

Haman was hung on the very same gallows he had built for Mordecai, who was promoted to Haman's position, and every Jewish person in the vast Persian Empire was delivered from certain death!

THIS ELECT LADY HUMBLED PHARAOH (THROUGH HER SON)

Two lesser-known Elect Ladies in the Scriptures risked their lives to protect God's anointed seed or children.

Jochebed's name rarely comes up in casual conversations, but without her, the Jewish people probably wouldn't exist today. This Elect Lady literally humbled Pharaoh through her son.

She married a grandson of Levi named Amram while she and all the rest of Jacob's descendants were still slaves of Pharaoh in Egypt.

They had two children, but before Jochebed learned that she was pregnant with her third child, Pharaoh suddenly announced a new "population control" plan. Her first two children, a boy and a girl, were old enough to be safe—but if the baby she carried was a boy, he would have to be killed by royal decree.

She conspired with the Jewish midwife to hide her son after he was born. When the boy grew too big to hide, Jochebed coated a basket or reed chest with tar and pitch and hid him among the reeds of the Nile River. Her daughter, Miriam, stayed behind to watch what would happen to him.

Pharaoh's daughter came to the river to bathe and found the basket among the reeds. That is when Miriam stepped forward to ask the princess if she wanted her to find a "Hebrew nurse" to nurse the boy for her.

Naturally, it was Jochebed who was hired by the Egyptian princess to nurse the boy (and raise her own infant son in safety). When Moses was weaned, Jochebed returned him to the Egyptian palace to be raised as a prince of Egypt. The rest is biblical history—but none of it would have happened if the Elect Lady named Jochebed had not defied the ruler of Egypt to preserve her son's life.

HANNAH'S PASSIONATE PRAYER INFLUENCED AN EMPIRE

As we noted earlier, Hannah was another Elect Lady anointed by God to persevere through most of her marriage as a woman unable to bear children—until she poured out her heart to God and vowed to give her child to Him if He would open her womb.

God quickly answered her prayer, and nine months later, Samuel was born. It was Samuel who brought reform to Israel and paved the way for David to ascend to the throne of Israel and Judah.

Again, history was made when one of God's Elect Ladies cried out in passionate prayer to Him in her pain. Her son, the prophet Samuel, birthed the existence of the Israelite empire through his ministry in establishing the rules of Saul and David. (See 1 Samuel.)

Toward the end of King David's life, one of his older sons decided to seize the throne of Israel early so none of the other princes could claim the crown. Prince Adonijah called military leaders, priests, political leaders, and friends to a coronation party. He revealed his ungodly motivations when he personally sacrificed sheep and cattle on a high place called "the Stone of the Serpent" without inviting any of King David's most loyal people.[2]

THE WISE KING MOVES ASIDE THE SERPENT KING

Bathsheba stepped in to warn King David about the plot and reminded him of a promise that Solomon would be king after him, and David agreed to act quickly. Solomon was crowned king over Israel even as the other prince was celebrating his self-proclaimed victory. (Perhaps this is a prophetic picture of God's wise king moving aside man's serpent king at a future time and place.)

Bathsheba covered her son and his destiny in God.

Bathsheba accepted her election as one of God's Elect Ladies and covered her son *and his destiny* in God, saving her nation from much grief. (See 1 Kings 1.)

After the death of David and Solomon, generations of kings in Israel and Judah led their people into the darkness of idol worship, child sacrifice, and sin. And once again, God used an Elect Lady to accomplish His purposes. He anointed a woman named Jehoshabeath to safeguard Joash from assassination for six long years. This was especially important because Joash was *David's only living male descendant.*

185

Jehoshabeath was the wife of a priest and the sister of Judah's king who had died in battle. The evil queen mother (Athaliah) wanted all power in her own hands, so she began to murder her own grandsons!

SHE SAVED DAVID'S HEIR FROM A MURDEROUS GRANDMOTHER

Even as this crazed grandmother killed her own grandsons, Jehoshabeath boldly snatched the youngest one, Joash, out from under Athaliah's nose and hid him in a bedroom. Jehoshabeath and her husband the priest hid Joash there for *six years* while his grandmother ruled Judah with an iron grip.

Finally, in Joash's eighth year, Jehoshabeath's husband, Jehoida, organized loyal leaders from among the Levites who armed themselves with weapons, surrounded the young king in a protective circle, and orchestrated a coup. Evil Athaliah was thrown out while Joash was put in. King Joash did well as long as Jehoshabeath and Jehoida were alive and in partnership with him. (See 2 Chronicles 22:10–24:2.)

Again, the destiny of a nation and the fulfillment of a divine prophecy hung in the balance, waiting for an Elect Lady who would risk her life to preserve God's chosen leader.

GOD IS STILL USING ELECT LADIES TODAY

God *still* uses His Elect Ladies to preserve His seed in our nation and around the world. Even as you read these words, thousands of very special women are sheltering young kings, deliverers, and prophets from destruction or abuse. Some of them even block deadly blows with their own bodies or step between their children and deadly harm, knowing they may never see their girlhood dreams come true.

If you are one of God's Elect Ladies, you should know something about God's attitude toward you. You are special and precious in His sight. There is something holy about people who willingly lay down their own comforts, dreams, and desires for the welfare of someone else.

It reminds me of Someone very special who left His throne and heavenly crown behind to set all of mankind free by laying down His own life for others. You are in good company. Keep the faith, keep your eyes on Jesus, and never give up! The Lord's next generation of worshipers and leaders is depending on you.

Be of good courage. This promise from God's Word applies to *you* right now:

> *God is not unjust, he will not forget your work and the love you have shown him as you have helped his people and continue to help them.* (Hebrews 6:10 NIV)

ENDNOTES

1. ABC News, "The Young Labeled 'Entitlement Generation'—The Entitlement Generation: Are Young Workers Spoiled or Simply Demanding a New Kind of Work Life?" by Martha Irvine, The Associated Press, June 26, 2005.

2. *"And Adonijah sacrificed sheep and oxen...by the **stone of Zoheleth**"* (1 Kings 1:9 NASB, emphasis added). *Zoheleth* means "gliding or serpent." The name indicates it was more than an odd geographic landmark; perhaps it had become an object of worship in opposition to the worship of Jehovah God. According to Merrill F. Unger, *Unger's Bible*

187

Dictionary, 3ʳᵈ ed. (Chicago: Moody Press, 1966), p. 1191, "*Zoheleth* [serpent, slippery] was a rocky and dangerous ledge or plateau 'by En-rogel' upon which Adonijah slew oxen and sheep. It overhangs the Kidron Valley."

About the Author

Eddie L. Long is the visionary and leader for New Birth Missionary Baptist Church. Since his installation in 1987, New Birth's membership has quickly multiplied from 300 to well over 25,000. In that time, Bishop Long directed numerous building expansions, land acquisitions, and building development efforts. These efforts led to the construction of a 3,700-seat sanctuary in 1991, a Family Life Center in 1999, and a 10,000-seat complex in 2001. He also serves as the founder and CEO of Faith Academy, New Birth's school of excellence. Located in the heart of DeKalb County, Georgia, in the city of Lithonia, New Birth Missionary Baptist Church continues to impact the community through countless outreach programs and community-empowering projects.

A native of North Carolina, Long received his bachelor's degree in business administration from

North Carolina Central University and a master's of divinity degree from Atlanta's Interdenominational Theological Center. Additionally, Long has received honorary doctorates from North Carolina Central University, Beulah Heights Bible College of Atlanta, and the Morehouse School of Religion.

Bishop Long is revered locally, nationally, and internationally as a dynamic man of vision, leadership, integrity, and compassion. He serves on an array of boards, including the Morehouse School of Religion Board of Directors, the Board of Visitors for Emory University, the Board of Trustees for North Carolina Central University, the Board of Trustees for Young Life, the Board of Trustees for Fort Valley State University, the Board of Directors for Safehouse Outreach Ministries, and the Board of Trustees for Beulah Heights Bible College. He is also an honorary member of the 100 Black Men of America. Bishop Long has been named one of America's 125 most influential leaders and has received a plethora of awards in recognition of his world-changing ministry.

In 2004, Bishop Long established a mentorship program known as the Longfellows Summer Academy to assist in the mental, physical, and spiritual development of young men between the ages of twelve and sixteen. What began as an eight-week program quickly developed into a lifelong commitment. And with this new commitment, Bishop Long began to raise funds earmarked for educational scholarships for the sixty-three charter members of the Longfellow Summer Academy.

Bishop Long's *Taking Authority* broadcast, which is seen in 170 countries worldwide, has received more than 40 nationally recognized honors. A noted author, Bishop Long's captivating and powerful messages are masterfully captured in a number of books, as well as audio and video series, including *I Don't*

Want Delilah, I Need You; The Spirit of Negativity and Familiarity and Kingdom Relationship; Power of a Wise Woman; What a Man Wants, What a Woman Needs; Called to Conquer; Gladiator: The Strength of a Man; Taking Over, and his most recent, *It's Your Time.*

Bishop Long and his wife, Vanessa, are the proud parents of four children: Eric, Edward, Jared, and Taylor. The couple has also served as surrogate parents for many other children in the church and community.

To contact Bishop Eddie L. Long, write, phone,
or visit him on the web at:

New Birth Missionary Baptist Church

P.O. Box 1019

Lithonia, GA 30058

770-696-9600

www.newbirth.org

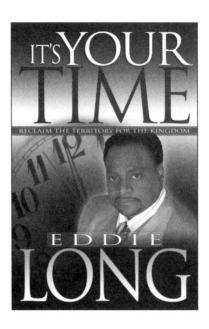

It's Your Time:
Reclaim Your Territory for the Kingdom
Eddie Long

Have we, as believers, allowed the world to silence us? By slowly eroding our rights to free speech…by passing laws saying that marriage isn't necessarily between a man and a woman…that murder is okay… that it's wrong to display the Ten Commandments… Is this really equality for all, except for Christians?

Join Eddie Long in reclaiming what has been lost. He will inspire you to rise up, take authority, and boldly assert your power as a believer. Discover how to redefine your life's purpose and vision while you raise your children to be godly leaders. Speak up, Christians! Now is the time for our unified voice to be heard, to take a stand together, and to stand firm. It's our time.

ISBN: 978-0-88368-783-3 • Hardcover • 192 pages

www.whitakerhouse.com